TRACKING THE ARK OF THE COVENANT

TRACKING THE ARK OF THE COVENANT

BY CAMEL, FOOT AND ANCIENT FORD

IN SEARCH OF

ANTIQUITY'S GREATEST TREASURE

CHARLES FOSTER

MONARCH
BOOKS

Oxford, UK & Grand Rapids, Michigan, USA

First published in the UK in 2007 by Monarch Books
(a publishing imprint of Lion Hudson plc),
Wilkinson House, Jordan Hill Road, Oxford, OX2 8DR.
Tel: +44 (0) 1865 302750   Fax: +44 (0) 1865 302757
Email: monarch@lionhudson.com
www.lionhudson.com

ISBN: 978-1-85424-800-8 (UK)
ISBN: 978-0-8254-6152-1 (USA)

Distributed by:
UK: Marston Book Services Ltd, PO Box 269, Abingdon, Oxon OX14 4YN.
USA: Kregel Publications, PO Box 2607, Grand Rapids, Michigan 49501.

Unless otherwise stated, Scripture quotations are taken from the Holy Bible, New Revised Standard Version,© 1989, 1995 by the Division of Christian Education of the National Council of the Churches of Christ in the United States of America.Used by permission. All rights reserved.

The Tolkien quotations on p. 19 and p. 23 are by kind permission of Harper Collins Publishers Ltd.

The text paper used in this book has been made from wood independently certified as having come from sustainable forests.

British Library Cataloguing Data
A catalogue record for this book is available from the British Library.

Printed and bound in Malta by Gutenberg Press.

To my mother,
who has sought for a long time,
and does not believe that she has found.

And to Tom,
whose joyful searching and finding in every second
have taught me so much about how to live.

These are the facts. What the truth is I do not know...

Amos Oz, *A Tale of Love and Darkness*

Contents

	Acknowledgments	11
	Preface	15
Chapter 1:	Beginnings	17
Chapter 2:	Setting the Course	25
Chapter 3:	Sand and Grit	49
Chapter 4:	Toward the Sunrising	67
Chapter 5:	Conquest	91
Chapter 6:	Consolidation and Captivity	109
Chapter 7:	Up to the Mountain	133
Chapter 8:	The Jewel in Sheba's Crown	147
Chapter 9:	Into the Ether	167
Chapter 10:	Epilogue	205
	Select Bibliography	211
	Index	213

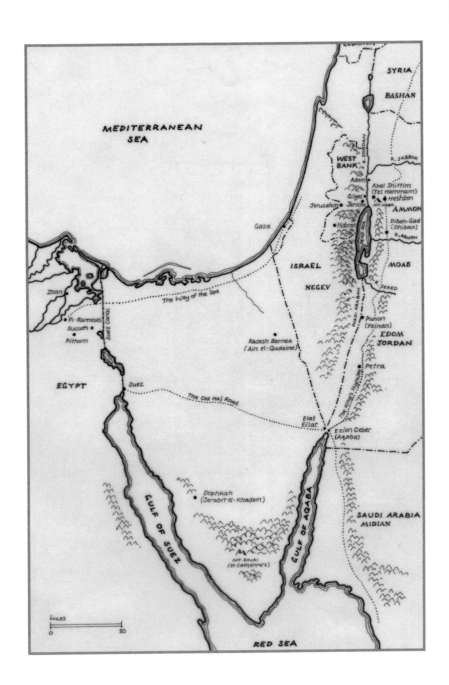

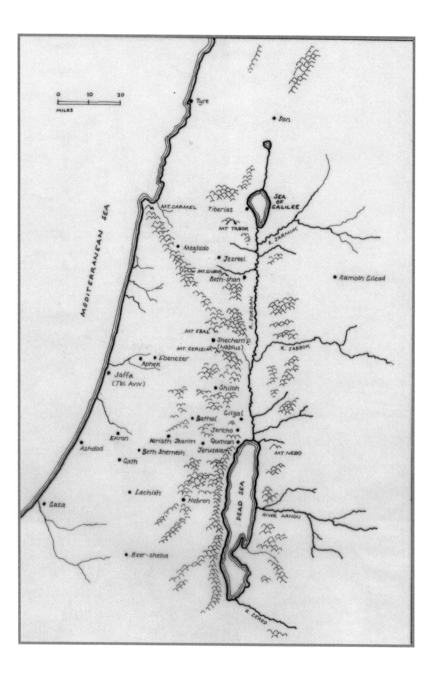

Acknowledgments

Every book is a mosaic of fragments from the lives and ideas of thousands of people. That is very obviously true of a travel book, which is a product of pure piracy. I am hugely grateful to all those people, known and unknown, who allowed me, and in many cases encouraged me, to board and plunder them.

Names are always invidious, but I have to mention:

In Egypt: Chris Beckingham, one my oldest and most faithful friends, who stuck by me while I was being even more than usually moody and difficult, and who said, improbably, that he'd enjoyed it all.

Dr Emma Loveridge, whose wisdom prevented a number of my trips to Sinai from being completely catastrophic.

The five Mohammeds, and Walid, Sa'id, Abdel, Rafiq, Samar and Salah, for their dignity, patience, courtesy and cheerfulness in the middle of a sea of burning grit.

Everyone at the Windsor Hotel, Cairo, the finest oasis either side of Suez.

And that Israeli with the mutilated hand — may you find what you are looking for.

In Jordan: Saleem and Ahmed, despite everything.

In Israel: Lee Glassman, Israel's best fixer and guide, and a thoroughly nice chap.

Ze'ev Erlich and Esti Herskowitz, who piloted me with skill, calm, erudition and gentle irony through the turbulent waters of occupied Samaria.

Aharon and Elika Barak, for matchless hospitality and inspiration over many years.

Joe Zias, the man who *is* Israeli forensic anthropology, for crawling with me through some of Jerusalem's strangest places; and his wife Levana, who is awesomely rumoured to be as good an interpreter of Aramaic inscriptions as she is a cook. I can vouch for her as a cook.

Professor Avi Faust, whose view of the ethnogenesis of Israel, generously given over tofu to the slowest student he's ever likely to teach, determined the colour of many central passages in this book.

Silvie Neumann, who infected me badly with her passion for the archaeology of the Philistine tels.

Leen Ritmeyer, a great archaeological draughtsman and a true gent.

Peter Wells, of The Garden Tomb Association in Jerusalem, for his perceptive audit of Ron Wyatt's strange career.

In Ethiopia: Keith Powell, with whom I've bled and moaned in some of the worst places on the planet.

In Ireland: That bloke shooting rabbits at Loughcrew.

In the USA: Dr Dennis Hillman, whose perceptive comments diluted *some* of the bumptiousness of the original manuscript.

And in the UK: Anne and Iain Norrie: most of this book was written in their house on Kintyre. They locked me into an upper room looking onto an Iron Age hill fort about the same age as many of the central events in the Ark's story. Their hospitality was amazing and sacrificial.

Tony Collins, Simon Cox and all the team at Monarch. There are no more congenial publishers.

James Wade, one of the most thoughtful and most erudite illustrators working today. His superb illustrations hugely enhance this book.

My wife Mary, who is my best friend and (even when she's not on the road with me) my fellow traveller.

Preface

It was a great arrogance to write this book. All I can say in mitigation is that I know a lot less than I did before I started.

Although it was arrogant, it was great fun. I love every single one of the places that I had to go to, apart from the Sinai and Coventry.

A really good Preface is important, particularly to the reviewers. But I can't write one. This isn't a book with conclusions that can be helpfully foreshadowed. It's a book about a journey from mystification to greater mystification. If it has a conclusion at all, it concludes – probably arrogantly again – that that journey amounts to some sort of progress. But the markers on the ground that allow progress to be measured are pretty obscure, and the dark is deep.

There is inevitably some recitation of Biblical stories. I have generally not included the reference: they would have cluttered up the text and are easy enough to find if anyone is interested.

I made a lot of friends when I was writing this book. Some of them appear in the Acknowledgments.

I also lost some friends. They are divided almost equally between those offended because I am too liberal and those offended because I am too conservative. To all of them I am very sorry for the hurt.

Charles Foster
London, March 2007

CHAPTER 1

Beginnings

Far over the misty mountains cold
To dungeons deep and caverns old
We must away ere break of day
To seek the pale enchanted gold.

J. R. R. Tolkien, The Hobbit

As I pushed open the gate to the church, a crow flapped heavily away to an elm copse across the valley. Warm rain fell, and I was sweating from the steep walk over the hill. There was not much light left. The drive from London had taken a lot longer than I'd planned: the traffic outside Oxford had been nightmarish.

On the chipped plaster by some medieval stained glass some figures were painted in ochre. Around them were some curious coils and swirls which, seen through a kabbalistic lens, said that beside a holy well, fifteen miles away, the Knights Templar had buried a great treasure that they had brought with them from Jordan.

The well had been wrecked by a road-widening scheme, but we drove to the place where it had been, took some bad photographs of an anonymous field, and went home.

That was the last bit of travelling.

It had all started in the Windsor Hotel, Cairo, which is the old British officers' club. I had just returned from Sudan, dusty, disillusioned, exhausted and frustrated. I had wandered for a flea-bitten fortnight across a waste of hot gravel, trying to feel heroic and significant. Even there I bunked down each night by a mess of Coke cans, and the Voice of America was pumped out into the village dark.

So, back in the Windsor, bathed, and with the ticks pulled out of my groin, I started to moan. I pointed to the hartebeest skull over the bar, and said that that was shot at a time when men were men; when there were real adventures to be had; when the world had not given up all her secrets. On the table next to me an Israeli with a mutilated hand looked up at me, swallowed a mouthful of hibiscus, put down his copy of Herodotus, and started to berate me. I was a fool, he said; and an arrogant, uneducated, ungrateful one too. What I had said showed that I had no eyes; that I was a spiritual down and out. Adventures were for the adventurous. I should get out of this country and back to the suburbs where I belonged. And as for him: well, he had sworn to stay on the road until he had tracked down the Ark of the Covenant.

I thought he was mad, and he probably was. But those last words burned away in my brain.

I knew the bare bones of the story. He was looking for the gold-covered wooden box made in Sinai during the Exodus. Some of the accounts read as if it were a box used to carry round God himself. It was said to contain the tablets of the law and (depending on which account you read) some of the manna given to the Israelites as food, the miraculous budding rod of Aaron, and sometimes other things too. The older the history, the emptier the box. By the time the New Testament talks about it, it is cluttered with relics of unapproachable sanctity. On its lid were two golden cherubim, and from between them God himself spoke. It stood at the centre of the camp at night, and guided the refugees during the day. It was lethal. Anyone who approached it without the proper obsequies died most horribly, and it was used as an apocalyptic weapon of mass destruction. But it was a most temperamental one.

After the Israelites found their way back home, they seem to have forgotten about the Ark for hundreds of years at a time. It gathered dust in a provincial shrine. It had its priests, but they were hardly big players in the Israelite national game. Then its fortunes changed. It was brought out in the hope that it could work a military miracle against the Philistines. Not only did it fail, but it fell into the enemy's hands. The story of what happened then is in this book. It is a story of disease, terror, calamity, gold and cows.

You would have thought that the Israelites would have learned that the Ark was not to be trifled with. And perhaps they did. Fear, neglect and downright bafflement shuffled the Ark between some shabby little bungalows outside Jerusalem. God was put into the Israelites' lumber-room. And then David, leaping and dancing in an ecstasy that got him ticked off by his staid family, brought the Ark up to Jerusalem. But even now the Ark, which had brought Israel home, had no home of its own. The home had to wait for Solomon. He built a temple which was deemed good enough. And so, on the Temple Mount, in the hot dark of the Holy of Holies, sprinkled with blood, the Ark stood in an incense cloud at the centre of the Jerusalem cult.

And so it remained until about 586 BC. Or *perhaps* it did. I knew that some said that it was spirited away to Ethiopia. Or (per Steven Spielberg) to Egypt. At any rate, in 586 BC the Babylonians burst into Jerusalem. Did they destroy the Ark? I knew that many thought they did not. But where was it? Did it return to Jerusalem when the Jews returned from their exile by the waters of Babylon? Did it stand in the inner sanctum of the rebuilt Temple? Was it carried off by the Greeks? Or the Romans? Or did it stay hidden, its location forgotten or known only to a tiny band of *cognoscenti*? Was it subsequently found?

There was, and is, no shortage of determined searchers. When you go to Jerusalem you can see tunnels dug by the Templars at the south end of the Temple Mount. This was systematic archaeological exploration by men who weren't doing it for a PhD. But what on earth were they looking for, and what did they find? I had read sensational modern head-lines about the Ark being found in Jerusalem's Garden Tomb, and in Jordan, Utah and Ireland.

After that withering and entirely just denunciation from the Israeli, I hardly slept. I turned these things neurotically over and over, then had a cold shower and got an early morn-ing cab from the Windsor to the airport. I wasn't going to be shamed into some absurd wild-goose chase around the Middle East. I had had enough sand and flies for a while. I was going to go home and write a book about the wildlife of the Outer Hebrides, and started to sketch it out in my head.

We stopped in a traffic jam on a flyover near the Khan al Khalili. As usual I was late for my flight, and was fuming as we stood for five minutes. We were opposite a huge cigarette advertising poster. It showed the artefact that confronted

Howard Carter when he peered into the ante-chamber of Tutankhamun's tomb: the wooden statue of the dog-god Anubis, sitting on the top of a gold casket. The casket had poles on either side so that it could be carried. It was an ark.

'Facts become history', wrote Tolkien in *The Fellowship of the Ring*. 'History becomes legend, and legend becomes myth.' And myths have a way of becoming journeys.

CHAPTER 2
Setting the Course

The travel writer is necessarily humiliated by his subject.
And that is a great place to start.

Adam Nicolson

The Greek Orthodox monastery of St Catherine's, at the foot of Jebel Musa – the traditional Mount Sinai – is one of the most comprehensively desecrated places on the planet. Every morning air-conditioned buses disgorge hundreds of scantily clad tourists. Playing Russian roulette with malignant melanoma, they stream through the low, ancient door, belching and chewing, and they giggle when they are handed robes to cover themselves up. It's all as numinous as Las Vegas.

A gaggle of tight-shorted Ukrainians fought to get into the charnel-house where the skulls of the monastery's monks are stacked. Presiding over his dead, looking sternly at those Ukrainian thighs, is the body of St Stephanos, fully clothed and wearing a purple cap.

There was a great rush for the burning bush – an orange-flowering shrub that occurs only rarely elsewhere. Cuttings from the monastery's own Bush are said to refuse to grow anywhere else. The cracks in the wall by the Bush are crammed with petitions on scraps of paper. It's a strange theology that does this.

Many were moved. The chewing had stopped. 'Just think, Dwight,' said a woman from deep Texas, close to tears. 'This is where it was. This is where our God' (by which she plainly intended to exclude the God of the Jews and the Muslims) 'spoke to Moses.'

Well, no, actually. Or at least, probably not.

Like many places in the Near East, Jebel Musa owes its fame, its desecration and its lively olive-wood-camel-based economy to Helena, the mother of Constantine. She was a frenetic collector of holy places who went busily round the Near East, identifying many sites as those referred to in the Bible. We don't know why she picked on Jebel Musa. There is no evidence of a pre-Byzantine identification. But if she intended to choose the most spectacular set for the dramatization of the Judaeo-Christian story, she could hardly have done better. Jebel Musa is one of the highest mountains in the central Sinai range. None of the other Sinai ranges would have done anything like as epic a job. The noon sun flattens the face of the mountain, ironing out all character other than forbidding solemnity. Between eleven and two the rock speaks of nothing but judgment. But when the sun dips, the mountain starts to shiver, the face melts, and if you want the mountain to preach at you, it is not hard to see judgment mitigated by a gentle, pastoral loveliness – a rounded, female beauty.

In other, less poetic ways, it fits the bill too. If you think that the Bible is right in apparently asserting that there were about two or three million in the Exodus, then you need a great plain in the lee of the mountain for them to camp on as they wait for Moses. And Jebel Musa has the perfect place: a huge natural campsite.

But although Jebel Musa has its scholarly proponents, they are a beleaguered minority. Many other sites are proposed: some in central Sinai, some in northern and eastern Sinai, some in the Negev, and some in Saudi Arabia. The identification of the site is rather important for this book: it was there, of course, that the Ark was made, and there that the journey proper starts. But it can't be done.

Moses was at Mount Sinai because he had an appointment there. It was an appointment made many years earlier. As an impetuous young man he killed a brutish Egyptian overseer who was beating an Israelite. Fearing for his life, he fled from Egypt and started a new life. That life was in Midian, where he married the priest's daughter. There is little controversy about the location of Midian: it was on the north-western coast of Saudi Arabia. However you fiddle with the location of Midian, it can't be exported across the Red Sea. It is not in Sinai, and never was.

One day Moses was pasturing his father-in-law's flock 'beyond the wilderness'. It was then that he came to Mount Horeb/Mount Sinai, and saw the burning bush. But where on earth was this? The difficulties of the text have led many to assume that it wasn't on earth at all – that it was a creature of the theological imagination. Certainly there are real difficulties, but there's no reason to throw out the historical baby with the theological bathwater.

The bus from Cairo disgorged us at a little cluster of huts on the edge of the Gulf of Aqaba. Behind us there was a great velvet wall of blood-red rock. In front of us, across the Gulf, the mountains of Midian swayed in the dying heat of the day. A Somali-registered ship, full of Jordanian cement, hooted out towards the Straits of Tiran. We put on masks and slipped into the water, and felt the throb of the propeller in our ears, and chased clown-fish into a forest of blue anemones. When we came out there was an icy moon. We lay on the sand and looked at Arabia. 'That's a long way to go to feed sheep,' said Chris.

It is perfectly true that, to this day, Bedouins go a long way to look for pasture. But no remotely intelligent Midian Bedou go to Sinai. Sinai is a long, long way, and, most importantly, it has at all material times been a dismal, dry desert. It would make far more sense, if one were dumped with a flock of hungry sheep in mid or south Midian, to drive them north or north-east (both of which would take you across an inhospitable wilderness, fitting nicely with the text) to the relatively green mountains of northern Midian. If that's right, then Mount Sinai is there.

There are other reasons for rejecting a Mount Sinai in Sinai. Many of the place-names in Midian match the stops in the exodus itineraries. The pillar of cloud by day, the pillar of flame by night, the clouds around the mountain-top, the trumpets and the shaking of the earth, sound compellingly like something volcanic. But there were no active volcanoes in Sinai at the time; there were in Midian. And there are some little textual clues – all the more compelling for their tiny incidentalness.

Here's one. The Israelites, famously, crossed the Re(e)d Sea, which drew back for them and then rolled onto the pursuing Egyptian army. Everyone knows the controversy about the translation of 'Red Sea'/'Reed Sea'. I am not going to enter the lists on either side. For these purposes it doesn't matter. In Hebrew the words are *Yam suph*. The exodus itineraries are an acquired literary taste, but here is something that anyone should get excited by. Put the Exodus and Numbers itineraries side by side. In Exodus 14:26–29 and Numbers 33:8, the Israelites miraculously cross the *Yam suph*. They are then in territory which has proved impossible to identify convincingly with anywhere in Sinai. In both accounts they go via Marah to Elim. Now here's the point. According to Numbers 33:10, they set out from Elim and camp by the *Yam suph*. That, note, is after they have crossed it once. There are then a few more stages, via Rephidim, to Mount Sinai. Look at the map. The accounts, read together, are consistent with two hypotheses: first, that the miraculous crossing was of the Gulf of Suez, and after crossing somewhere near the modern Suez Canal, the Israelites turned south and then east; or, second, that the miraculous crossing was of the Gulf of Aqaba (perhaps somewhere near modern-day Eilat/Aqaba), and that the refugees then turned south, along the Red Sea coast, towards Midian. If the first is right, they were moving mighty slowly for a people running for their lives. If the second is right, they were moving rather fast. I know which version I'd tend to believe.

But is there no way of testing this? Can archaeology not help in locating Mount Sinai? The answer is that it has not helped, and may not be able to help. Nomads generally do leave traces, and it is often possible to find those traces 3,500 or more years later, but the traces are often subtle. You need to know where to look. And to know where to look you need a consistent tradition (which no one has); a clear documentary record (which doesn't exist); a huge amount of luck (so far elusive to all serious researchers); or divine guidance. Which brings us to the tale of Ron Wyatt.

If you believe even a fraction of what he claimed, Wyatt, a bearded Seventh Day Adventist nurse from Tennessee, was easily the most successful archaeologist who has ever lived. He claimed to have found Noah's Ark and the true sites of Golgotha, Sodom and Gomorrah, and to have solved the mystery of how the pyramids were built. He also found time to locate the Red Sea crossing, Mount Sinai and finally the Ark of the Covenant itself. Of which more later.

In 1978 Ron Wyatt first went to Nuweiba, that port on the Gulf of Aqaba from which Chris and I had looked out towards Midian. He seems to have been immediately convinced that this was the place where the Israelites crossed the Red Sea. This was on the basis, apparently, that the beach was big enough to hold the biblical multitudes and their flocks, and that escape from the south end of the beach would have been impossible – so fitting a comment by Josephus to the effect that Pharaoh's army enclosed the Israelites 'between the inaccessible precipices and the sea…where the [ridges of] the mountains were closed with the sea…' So he put on his scuba gear and went in to have a look around. Things tended to happen immediately for Ron Wyatt: '…on his first dive at the site, [Ron] found chariot remains… They were covered in coral, which made it difficult to see them clearly, but it appears that the coral was the agent the Lord used to preserve them…' The wheels have never been submitted for analysis.

The next stage was just as easy. Wyatt turned to some maps of the region that the Israelites would have crossed. He quickly decided that Jebel el Lawz, in north-western Saudi Arabia, was the obvious candidate for Mount Sinai, and applied to the Saudi embassy for a visa to visit. The embassy didn't bother to reply, and after being assured that the Saudis were positively hospitable towards illegal immigrants, Wyatt went to Jordan with his sons Danny and Ronny and simply walked undetected across the Saudi border. They hitch-hiked and hired taxis to the Jebel al Lawz area, and again luck, or God, was immediately on their side. Wyatt saw some marble pillars lying on the ground. He opened his Bible, and there was the explanation. According to the Book of Exodus, Moses had set up twelve pillars near his Sinai altar – one pillar for each of the tribes. And there they were. Next to them were the remains of the altar, and engraved on the stones was an Egyptian-style picture of a cow; this, of course, was the altar of the famous Golden Calf. Nearby was the split rock from which Moses smote water. Everything else fitted too: the summit of the mountain was charred, and there was a natural amphitheatre surrounded by peaks, making the perfect Hollywood backdrop for those dramatic Mosaic speeches.

It was the archaeological coup of the last four millennia. But there was yet more. As they tried to leave the country, Wyatt and his sons were arrested, imprisoned and charged with espionage. Even this was a blessing, because some of their interrogators were convinced, and one day they took Wyatt in a helicopter back to the area to investigate his claims. They landed on the beach directly opposite Nuweiba, and there, just by the helicopter, was a previously undiscovered Phoenician-style granite column with, of course, an archaic Hebrew inscription.

Sprung from the Saudi jail, and back home in Nashville, Wyatt received a phone call from a Saudi national who said that he was a close relation of the King. He had heard about Wyatt's discoveries and was fascinated. He hadn't been able to eat or sleep: he had to see the holy mountain for himself. Would Wyatt return to Saudi Arabia and show him?

So in 1985 Wyatt went back. He showed the Saudis everything he had seen before. A Saudi archaeologist, unfortunately anonymous, shook Wyatt's hand: 'This is a major discovery,' he said. The Saudis were all convinced that this was the true mountain of Moses, and begged Wyatt to stay and excavate the site. Wyatt sadly had to decline; he was due in Ankara for an important meeting about the Noah's Ark project. The imperious Saudis, not used to being disobeyed, turned nasty. All the videos and photographs confirming the findings were confiscated. 'You are to forget that you ever came here,' Wyatt was told. 'We don't want to read about this in a book or see it in a movie.'

The book that unveiled Jebel al Lawz as the real Mount Sinai was not Wyatt's but Larry Williams'. Wyatt says that Williams and Bob Cornuke, following his directions, simply retraced his steps and described what he had found.

I am deeply uncomfortable about finding myself in the company of Ron Wyatt. He was no archaeologist, his assertions about the Ark of the Covenant – made in the same plausible, matter-of-fact drawl with which he spoke about Pharaoh's chariot wheels – are demonstrably false, and in most circumstances I would regard any archaeological assertion by him as compelling evidence for exactly the opposite. But the idea that Mount Sinai is in Saudi Arabia makes a good deal of sense.

If the Midian hypothesis is right, then it is not hard to work out which road the Israelites took from Egypt. It is a road I have taken many a time – the old Haj road running from Suez more or less to Aqaba, with a modern blip caused by the inconvenient interposition of Israel.

It was not a bad road in those days. Lawrence of Arabia rode from Aqaba to Suez in three days, if you believe him, and things hadn't changed much between the late Bronze Age and the First World War. But, most importantly, it was a remote road. The road across the top of the Sinai peninsula, by the Mediterranean, is easily the most direct way between Egypt and the Promised Land. But it has been an imperially policed motorway for most of known history. Certainly during Pharaonic times it was dotted with Egyptian forts. Moses would have been mad to lead the Israelites that way. They would have been arrested at the first checkpoint. He would also have missed that appointment at Mount Sinai. And indeed the Bible is clear: they didn't go that way.

The other option is the coast road up the Gulf of Suez. True, it wasn't as well policed as the northern road, but there was a fair amount of Egyptian traffic on it, going to and from the turquoise mines at Serabit el Khadem, and to the ports at the southern end of the peninsula which shipped in from Arabia a lot of the aromatic resin and incense so central to Pharaonic life and death. Today that Suez road is a big, bounding road: a queasy chain of blind summits between heaps of white sand and derelict filling stations. The Gulf is mottled, and sways, and at night is aflame with the flares of the rigs.

If the Israelites took the Haj road, I know what it would have been like. Today it is a fly-struck strip of sand and grit.

Every few miles there are bored conscripts in concrete pill-boxes, belligerently picking their noses. From the canal zone the road makes a last attempt at interest and significance, winding through some black, dogtooth mountains, before giving up like the rest of the landscape and settling down to the dead, flat monotony of burning central Sinai. Later the land rallies, and pushes up the odd acacia, and in the distance there are dark canyons. But still there is the same shimmering listlessness, where the only movement is mirage and the heaving of your own chest.

But there is water. Not much, and not of very good quality, but it is there. That is why the road is there. Many of the breeze-block settlements where we stopped to pick up hummus, *fuul* and campylobacter are built on the ruins of little caravanserai where pilgrims could water their camels, their donkeys and themselves. There's not enough water for three million people, though.

Outside the Orthodox Jewish community there are few serious scholars who contend these days for the literal truth of the Old Testament enumeration of the refugees. The account says that the total number of men, twenty years old or more, able to serve in the army, was 603,550. When women, children and the elderly are added in, you get to a figure of 2–4 million. You get to 3 million simply by assuming, very conservatively, a wife and three children per family.

The Bible's figure cannot be right. The Bible itself hints as much. It seems that there were only two Hebrew midwives – Shiprah and Puah – an impossibly small number for such a vast population. And the Bible makes a point of saying that the numbers involved in the Exodus were small. 'It was not because you were more numerous than any other people that the Lord set his heart on you and chose you', insisted Moses, according to the author of Deuteronomy. 'For you were the fewest of all peoples.'

The small numbers gave explicit cause for concern at the time of the conquest of Canaan. Indeed, those numbers dictated God's strategy for conquest: 'Little by little I will drive [the occupying peoples] out from before you, until you have increased and possess the land.' An Israelite army of 600,000-plus would have been the most formidable anywhere in the ancient world. If Herodotus is right (and he was a man who never knowingly underestimated anything), it would have dwarfed the Egyptian army, and it would certainly have brushed aside, as an elephant brushes a gnat, the Amalekites who gave the Israelites such a nail-bitingly anxious time at Rephidim. There would have been no need for Moses to go humbly, cap in hand, to the tinpot kingdom of Edom, asking for safe passage. Indeed, there would have been no need for the supernatural Exodus epic at all. The Israelites, if they could have fitted into the Delta where the Bible puts them, could simply have downed tools and wandered off whenever they wanted: there was no one in the Near East who could have stopped them. The 600 chariots that the Bible says were despatched by Pharaoh to stop the runaways would have been pathetically inadequate: the Israelites would have laughed at them and engulfed them.

Such a massive movement of people would certainly have left some extra-biblical trace in the historical record. You can edit some national embarrassments out of history, but nothing as tectonic as that. The best estimate of the entire population of Egypt during the Ramesside period is about 3.5 million. Colin Humphreys (himself a faithful conservative

Christian) elegantly and definitively disposes of the traditional view: the Book of Numbers tells us that the total number of firstborn males a month or more old was 22,273. If this figure is correct, what follows? In ancient civilizations about half the population was under twenty. Say then (and it is conservative), that the total number of Israelite men of all ages was about a million. The average mother must have had about fifty sons and fifty daughters. It didn't happen.

But it is not, in fact, the Bible that has it wrong. It is the translators. The figures rest on the translation of a Hebrew word, *eleph*, as 'a thousand'. It often does mean this, but it can also mean 'group', 'clan' or 'military unit'. The various extrapolations from this retranslation are complex, but what it comes to is this: the numbers involved in the Exodus were in the thousands. It may have been a few tens of thousands. It got nowhere near hundreds of thousands.

Disillusioned by the morning tour buses, and desperate for a noseful of the odour of sanctity I'd inhaled at other Orthodox monasteries, I walked at dusk back up the road to St Catherine's monastery. It was a still, close evening. The rocks were blood red and the buttresses of the mountain teetered vertiginously into the deep blue. I caught the edge of the scent from the cypresses in the monastery garden, and began to see why men who wanted to get to the bottom of things would choose to come here, even if it meant being holed up in their burrows between nine and twelve every day, while the world surged around them.

Then, walking down the road towards me, I saw a rotund, black-cloaked monk, his hair knotted in an ecclesiastical ponytail, his beard down to his navel. Here was my chance to ask about the connection with the great Orthodox citadel of Mount Athos, from which many of the monks had come.

'Good evening, Abuna,' I said.

He smiled and nodded acknowledgment. But he could not have heard me because of the Phil Collins that was playing deafeningly on his MP3. I went back to town.

In the hot streets of St Catherine's village most of the shops were still shuttered for Ramadan, and most of the people were behind the shutters, either fasting or keen not to be seen not fasting. A dog snapped at flies. The angry young preacher at the mosque berated and exhorted and threatened, but the people who listened to it were tired and impassive. His great waves of words rolled along the valley bottom towards the monastery, and seeped through the bolted fifth-century door. When the preacher stopped, and the crowds slouched back to their dark rooms, the radio was flicked on at the telephone bureau, and a faster, hotter voice from Medina crackled out, urgent and hard – like an excited football commentary, but without the joy.

A new Islam is rising in Egypt and throughout the Middle East: a strident, merciless, unlettered Islam; an Islam that would have poured napalm on the hanging gardens of Cordoba; a very un-Egyptian and very un-Islamic Islam.

In less than a generation the generally happy coexistence (and sometimes symbiosis) of Islam and Christianity in the Middle East is being fatally threatened. When the Pope incautiously cited (albeit in huge inverted commas) a four-teenth-century emperor who spoke of Islamic belligerence, furious Islamic radicals took to the streets; convents were torched; priests were killed. The English satirical magazine *Private Eye* ran a cartoon showing two Muslims speaking:

'How dare they say we're violent,' said one. 'Yes. Let's kill them,' said the other.

This, along with all other ironies and nuances, was of course wholly wasted on the radicals. And here's another irony: they talk about President Bush's crusade against Islam. US policy has undoubtedly made the plight of Middle Eastern Christians far worse, but the ancient Christian communities have been unequivocal in their denunciation of the US. Nonetheless, they find themselves the victims of a true crusade: an Islamic crusade to rid the Middle East of the Christians who, remember, were long established here before the Prophet was born.

The crusade is effective. There is a massive haemorrhage of Christians from the region. It is estimated that the remaining Arab Christians in Jerusalem could be evacuated in five jumbo jets. Soon the Byzantine monasteries of the Middle East will be museums, and the only Christian worshippers in Jerusalem will have stepped off planes from Atlanta.

'What are you here for?' asked the boy who brought us our tea.

'We're looking for the Ark of the Covenant,' Chris replied.

'The Ark of the Covenant?' spat the boy. 'That's a fairy tale for the Jews.'

The following day we holed up in the hotel. I read and re-read the accounts of the building of the Ark. If it is a fairy tale, it is a very strange and explicit one.

The Ark story is part of a series of episodes at Mount Sinai in which Jahweh tells the Israelites quite a lot about himself and about their relationship to him. Moses makes a number of trips up the mountain. There he meets with Jahweh, who tells him that he is going to enter into a contract with the Israelites. If they keep their part of the bargain, they will be his 'treasured possession out of all the peoples…a priestly kingdom and a holy nation.' The people agree to be obedient, and then the law is given. Moses takes the people out of their camp to meet Jahweh. They stand at the foot of the mountain, which is wrapped in smoke. Smoke goes up from it 'like the smoke of a kiln'. The whole mountain shakes, and there is a trumpet blast 'so loud that all the people trembled'. Jahweh says that the mountain is unapproachably holy: even to touch it will mean death. Then the law is given, and it is terribly stern. First come the Ten Commandments, but in the same breath other commandments follow, with apparently the same binding, universal, eternal authority, that cause more problems to the modern mind. Slavery appears to be specifically endorsed; anyone who curses his father or mother is condemned to death; the owner of a homicidal ox with a record of goring is likewise to be killed, together with female sorcerers and people who commit sexual offences with animals. There is a lot of death around. If this is a merciful God showing his nature, his is a severe mercy. Holiness is a terrible thing.

Just before I left for Egypt, I was walking through Leeds. An unhappy-looking man with a Belfast accent and an unnecessary raincoat pushed a leaflet into my hand. It urged me to join a demonstration outside Parliament to contend for 'Bible Truth'. I had missed my train, was in no rush, and had just been reading Leviticus, so I asked him what he meant.

'We want the Truth of Scripture to govern our nation,' he said, with audible capitals.

'So you want religious courts to replace secular judges, homosexuals to be stoned, and the death penalty for Sabbath breakers?' I asked.

'I can see that you sit in the seat of the Mockers and Scoffers,' he said, and turned on his heels and walked off to disseminate Truth to Those who Have Ears and are Ready to Hear.

But it was a real question. I genuinely didn't understand. I can see the logic – although I deplore the morality – of the Christian Taliban who tear down pagan monuments and would kill the farm labourer caught in a compromising position behind his cow. At least they're being consistent. It is not that I think the Bible is untrue: far from it. I'm just not clear why I should denounce civil partnerships for homosexuals but not burn witches or stone to death people who gather sticks on a Sunday.

But in the middle of the rumbling dark, at the heart of the laws that speak of blood and vengeance, there is something that looks very like love. Jahweh seems keener to bless than to smite. The jealousy is that of a mother who snatches her child violently from a predatory paedophile.

Then comes the Ark story. It is too familiar to us. In fact it is an immensely surprising twist. Jahweh has handed down the law. A trembling people has received it from a terrified Moses. And now, suddenly, Jahweh says that he is not going to stay on the summit of Mount Sinai. He is going to come along on the journey. And he is going to come in a box.

This idea must have met with a mixed reception. Some must have thought that it was rather like taking the headmaster away on holiday: the rules would be policed with uncomfortable diligence. They would get away with nothing. Others would have been glad that they had a captain of unquestionable power and authority to steer them through the rocks to port in Canaan.

So the Ark was made, to detailed specifications dictated by Jahweh, by a craftsman called Bezalel. The basic structure was of acacia wood, and it was overlaid, inside and outside, with pure gold. The Israelites had plenty of gold: it was thrust urgently into their hands by the terrified Egyptians. The Ark had four gold rings, through which went gold-covered acacia carrying-poles. On the lid, which formed the 'Mercy Seat', two cherubim, again of hammered gold, faced one another. The wings of the cherubim spread out over the Mercy Seat.

Cherubim appear once before in the Bible. They guarded the entrance to Eden, preventing man's return after his expulsion. This entrance was on the east side of Eden. The entrance to the Tabernacle, where the Ark spent its nights, was always to the east. The message was clear enough: access to God had been lost at the Fall, but Jahweh had taken the initiative and was brokering a peace. He would speak to Moses from the Mercy Seat. Relations were gradually being restored.

Was there only one Ark? It has sometimes been suggested that there were two or more. We come to the issue later, but the Bible is clear enough. There was most emphatically one Ark for emphatically One God.

Arks were two a shekel in the ancient world. There are plenty of examples from Egypt and Mesopotamia, and at least until recently, some of the Bedouin of the Hejaz carried Ark-like objects swaying on camelback beneath a canopy. They often had some cultic significance, as the Anubis ark from the cigarette advertisement did. There is nothing very unusual about the design of the Exodus Ark. Any Ramesside Egyptian would immediately have recognized it for what it was. The only comment that would probably have been passed was that it was rather plain. Pharaonic arks tend to be gorgeously decorated, often with scenes showing the triumph of the king's armies, or with theological friezes giving instructions about how to negotiate the treacherous waters of the afterlife. The importance of the Exodus Ark lay not in what was on the outside, but in what was on the inside and who could be met with on the lid.

Inside the Ark were the tablets upon which the Ten Commandments were written. The Ark was rather like a lawyer's vault, and indeed the writer of Deuteronomy implies that that was all it was. It contained the evidence of the relationship that had been sealed at Sinai. There were two sets of tablets, of course. The first was smashed by Moses in a fit of holy anger after the Israelites had proved faithless in the Golden Calf incident. There is no biblical suggestion that the broken tablets found their way into the Ark alongside the second, intact set, although a much later rabbinic tradition insists that they did. The Hollywood imagination has Moses staggering down the mountain under the weight of an elaborately carved masterpiece of monumental masonry. This is archaeological nonsense. Thin stone slivers were commonly used throughout the Near East to bear inscriptions. There wasn't a lot to write. If Moses had pockets in his *jalabiya*, the tablets could probably have been put easily into them as he clambered down. The tablets were later joined by Aaron's rod – the demonstration of the legitimacy of the priestly line, and the vindication of the priestly mode of commerce between man and God.

Pharaonic arks weren't dangerous, but this one was. It was lethal. To look on it, to touch it, or even to minister before it in a sincere but inappropriate way, meant death. It seems to have been indiscriminate in its lethality. Aaron's sons, Nadab and Abihu, no doubt from the best of motives, offered fire in a non-prescribed way. The result was deadly: '…fire came out from the presence of the Lord and consumed them, and they died before the Lord.' Like a holy infection, it was penned inside a sterile area, called the Tabernacle, from which all but the priests were rigorously excluded. Even this was not enough. At the centre of the Tabernacle, behind a curtain worked (in echoes of Eden) with cherubim, was the Ark's own enclosure: the Tent of Meeting. There Moses met with Jahweh and received the instructions which were relayed to the people.

Being a priest was a high-risk occupation. The priests (initially Aaron and his sons) had very detailed instructions about the protective clothing they were to wear. A whole chapter of Exodus deals with it. A good deal of that chapter describes the Breastplate, into which was set a complex array of highly specified stones.

All this specificity has led to speculation about what the Ark was. Some say it was a massive battery, built by Moses, schooled in Egyptian magic–science. In the National Museum of Baghdad there is (or was; it's probably been looted and sold on to a Moscow dealer by now) a small clay jar with a copper tube protruding into it. Down the tube hangs an iron rod. If you fill it with any acidic liquid (wine vinegar will do very well), you have a battery. Whether it was used that way in antiquity is disputed, but its antiquity is not. It's a Parthian device, dating from about 200 BC.

Others say that the Ark was a radioactive source. Look at the Bible carefully, they say. Isn't it odd that Moses' face didn't shine, and didn't need to be veiled, after the trip up the mountain to get the first set of tablets? And why did he smash them? Wasn't that a bit petulant? Surely they were smashed because, whatever they were, they didn't work. On the second trip up into the radioactive laboratory of Mount Sinai he got the formula right. Then the radioactive tablets did work and his face shone. Why did Moses say that no one should approach the mountain? Because all that radioactivity meant that it was dangerous, of course; and probably because he wanted to be left alone to work on his magic box. The thick gold of the Ark is a well-known baffle to radiation; the High Priest's Breastplate clearly had a similar function – it must have worked like a modern radiographer's lead apron.

This view of Moses and the Ark just doesn't work. If the Ark was some magician's box designed to enable Moses to control the people, it plainly failed. The story of the Exodus is the story of rebellion and disobedience. Moses doesn't wield the Ark as a wonder-working trickster would. And he is the most improbable hero. By the time the Exodus comes, he's an elderly, lisping murderer-on-the-run, so tongue-tied that his brother has to do most of his public speaking for him. And then at the end of the story there's no triumphant procession into the Promised Land, borne on the shoulders of his grateful people. He gets a frustrating glimpse at what he's been aiming for, and then dies and is buried in an unmarked grave. No author would ever have made Moses up. Pour all the cold water you want on the Old Testament documents; highlight gleefully all the manifest inconsistencies between the accounts. You're still left with Moses. He's too solid and too theologically uncomfortable to be pure fancy.

This is meant to be a travel book. Travel books are meant to be structurally easy to write. You travel, and then you write about where you've been. There's inevitably an inner journey too, and so some unavoidable autobiography. And, since straightforward landscapes are unreadably dull, there are always other layers: history, politics, anthropology and so on. The journey's the skeleton. But here is the problem with starting this book: until the Ark is poised on the edge of the Promised Land, about to take Joshua triumphantly through the Jordan, the Israelites' route is legendarily obscure. And in Sinai itself the obscurity is impenetrable.

It is best to state the facts brutally. There is no archaeological evidence whatever that the fleeing Israelites were ever in Sinai. The Bible's Exodus itinerary is very explicit. In fact it occurs more than once, and there are discrepancies between the various versions which are not easy to resolve. Despite the biblical detail, there is only anything approaching a consensus in the identification of a single site: Kadesh Barnea. The Israelites seem to have been there or thereabouts for quite a time during the Exodus. Some say that the bulk of the forty years was spent there. It was from there that they sent out their scouts into the Promised Land; the scouts who returned groaning under the weight of grapes from near Hebron, singing about a land flowing with milk and palm honey. There is broad agreement in the respected journals that Kadesh Barnea is modern-day Ain-el Quiderat in eastern Sinai, very near the border with Israel. Yet even there there is energetic and coherent dissent, in which I join.

The consensus about Kadesh Barnea increases rather than diminishes the problem for the biblical fundamentalists. For not one trace – not one single shard – from the times generally thought to be relevant has been recovered from there. It is not for want of looking.

So what is a writer to do? There is nothing he can do except marinade himself in the desert and say what it feels like.

CHAPTER 3
Sand and Grit

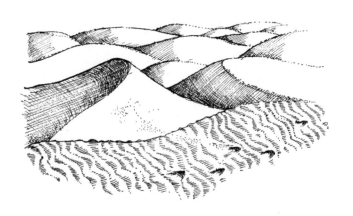

The Israelites set out from the Desert of Sinai and travelled from place to place until the cloud came to rest in
the Desert of Paran...

Numbers 10:12

For years we lived anyhow with one another in the naked
desert, under the indifferent heaven. By day the hot sun
fermented us; and we were dizzied by the beating wind.
At night we were stained by dew, and shamed into petti-
ness by the innumerable silences of stars...

T. E. Lawrence, *Seven Pillars of Wisdom*

...the path [of a desert hermit] could only be travelled by
one who was very alert and very sensitive to the land-
marks of a trackless wilderness. The hermit tends to be a
man mature in faith, humble and detached from himself
to a degree that is altogether terrible. The spiritual cata-
clysms that sometimes overtook some of the presumptuous visionaries of the desert are there to show the dangers
of the lonely life – like bones whitening in the sand.

Thomas Merton, *The Wisdom of the Desert*

I have spent a long time in Sinai. I have wandered through most parts of it; sometimes on my own; more usually with a single Bedouin guide. On one three-week traverse of the peninsula — a time of crushing loneliness and emetic self-examination — the sand and the rock broke my heart and nearly my mind. It took an extraordinary tenderness to restore them.

So I fear Sinai most terribly. I fear the brutal clarity with which you see yourself in the shimmering air. I fear the silence that shouts. It is too big and too high for me. I loathe the desert, and Sinai in particular. I have come here season after season, using it to beat out some warp in myself. But it is a blunt instrument, and it has always made some other part bend, or cause a fracture-line to develop.

I hate everything about it apart from the dreams of lushness and lemonade that it produces. I hate those interminable hot lunchtimes that start at 10.30 and end at 3 p.m.; where there's nothing to do but watch the flies and plan the logistics of the next bowel movement. I hate the busy, intent camel-ticks that race for your legs; I hate the little itchinesses that you welcome because at least they're a change from the other two competing sensations of boredom and fatigue. I hate the sour belching of the camels; I hate the spikiness of the leaves and the feminine curves of the dunes. And even, shamefully, I hate the brave little things that live here. I hate my own lectures about the ingenuity of their kidneys and about how they use seeds in their burrows to absorb the water exhaled as they sleep. I hate the fact that I can't see them as anything other than bits of furry engineering in a sea of hot grit. I hate them for bothering with life here, when I can't be bothered.

So I hate everything that belongs here. I like it best in the autumn and winter when I can look up and see the high clouds of storks or honey buzzards or passerines gusting south or north. If it is autumn they will be in Ethiopia within the week. If it is spring the storks will soon be on the chimneys of Hungary. There is a lot of comfort in this. It is some comfort, too, to know that the kite circling over our patch of desolation could angle a wing and see the waves, bright with phosphorescence, crashing into a happier kind of sand at Nuweiba. Yet sometimes, looking through the photos at home, I have seen beauty, and known it was no artefact of the light, and been frightened at my blindness.

The Israelites, in any event, loathed the desert. They complained like mad, and dreamt of steak and gardens. God didn't intend them to like it: it was a school, and it no doubt did them good. He had made them for a garden.

The modern Israelites, by and large, dislike the desert too. They try to extinguish it. They fill it with water and crops. If they like the desert, it's only because it shows in more impressive relief the colours of their plantations: green is more luscious against a background of white sand. Even when the desert is agriculturally irredeemable, the urge to tame persists: they dissect, explore, classify and describe, making it bloom archaeologically, geologically or zoologically.

Amongst the psychiatrically normal population there are three types of desert lovers. First, those whose immense capacity for introspection has allowed them to stamp on all their demons, and who can look at the emptiness and say:

'The lack of clutter lets me get on with what's really important.' These are real, rare, advanced saints, and I have never
knowingly met one. Then there are those with no capacity
for introspection, who are happy to say: 'I was born here,
and so was my father. He liked that rock, and so do I. And
there's plenty of tea and a goat on Friday night.' The Bedouin
are a dazzlingly unpoetic people. They have ghosts and feuds
and primary colours, but nuance can't survive in the temperatures of central Sinai. And then there are the people who
know nothing about the desert: the romantics. Towards the
end of Bruce Feiler's (very good) book *Walking the Bible*, he
meets, in an Amman office, the grandson of Auda Abu Tayeh,
the hook-nosed belligerent of Wadi Rum who rode with
Lawrence on Aqaba. Feiler describes how Abu Tayeh came
alive when the desert was mentioned. Feiler had had his own
desert epiphany, and the two men felt passing between them
the electricity of mutually acknowledged spiritual brotherhood. I'm deeply suspicious. Saturday picnics in an air-conditioned Land Cruiser in the Wadi Arabah are no doubt a
good thing, but desert-dwelling they are not.

There are, of course, many desert-o-paths. Englishmen
are over-represented amongst them, but Germans, French,
Swiss and Scandinavians are prominent too. Lawrence is their
High Priest: Doughty, Burton and Burckhardt are his
acolytes. For these men the desert is a diagnostic or thera-
peutic tool: a lamp to show them the writhings inside; a whip
to thrash the Self (usually pleasurably) into some sort of sub-
mission. And if you *use* something like that, you don't properly love it. Lawrence's wanderings weren't about the desert,
they were about Lawrence. The desert was an onanistic
device.

I went back to Sinai with Chris, and that was more or less fine. Everything tends to be all right with him. He's a trooper and a poet and a lover of steak-and-kidney pie, and we'd collected moths together as boys in Yorkshire. He stopped those sandstone buttresses nudging me out into despair, and I must have driven him mad. But when we got back to Cairo what he said was: 'Great trip. Really enjoyed it. It's odd that the Arabs eat so much tinned tuna. Cheers.'

The idea with Chris was to do some shuffling round south-central and eastern Sinai with some camels and a couple of Bedou chaps, passing through Ain El Quiderat (which might, just might, be the biblical Hazeroth, where Miriam was made into a leper, as white as snow, for bitching against Moses' Cushite wife), snatching photos and adjectives as we went. And that is what we did. There is no point in telling the route or the times. The desert conflates. That is its main use to mystics: it abolishes the distinctions between things, and that includes days, weeks and experiences.

The way it was for us was the way it was for Moses. When he travelled, the day began in the night. Usually there is a wind at night, because as the sky sucks the day's heat upwards it takes some air with it, and the air ruffles your mind as you sleep. And if there is no wind a heavy shroud of clotted air rests over every body lying on the goat-hair blankets around the fire, and presses the sleep out of you. The camels are restless, because there is a jackal in the wadi, and you can feel their unease rolling towards you. If there is a moon, the night is brighter than the dusk; the moon stings your eyes. Only the Bedou are not watchful. Their sleeping brains know the difference between a dazzling moon and the first touches of dawn. If you have pitched camp away from a flash-floodable wadi, there are no dangers here that anyone can do anything about. The modern Amalekites are the Al Qu'aida groups rumoured to train in eastern Sinai, but if you stay out of urban clubs they are unlikely to bother you, and if they did it wouldn't help to lie awake clutching your torch.

The stillness just before dawn is deeper than the stillness of the night. The land seems to be bracing itself for the impact of the sun. Then the camp, as if it has been thawed, starts to rattle and jingle, and as the heat seeps into the flies and geckos and snakes, they stretch and start to move, and the birds untuck their heads and look down from the ledges. We are always up before dawn, checking each other's backs for ticks, writing down the hot dreams that always breed in tepid sleep, and photographing frantically before the sun levels the land.

The Bible is extremely detailed in its descriptions of how Jahweh's service needed to be performed. The clothes are all specified; the means of atonement for a man who has had sexual intercourse with a female slave are set out; there is a linguistically obscure edict against beard-trimming. But there is no clear timetable for daily devotions; no day in the life of the Tabernacle and the Ark. This seems to be because the Ark, standing in the centre of the camp, was a living, dictating thing. It was the command centre of the camp, and it handed down bespoke directions to Moses. If it said that the Israelites should move, they moved.

Breakfast for Moses was manna, which looked like coriander seed, was the colour of gum resin, and, once it had been boiled and made into cakes, tasted like 'cakes baked with oil'. It went off so quickly that he was told not to keep it to the next day.

There is a huge literature on what manna was. It is

commonly taken to be the dried sap exuded by tamarisk trees when they are infested by particular species of plant lice, and this is still gathered by the Bedouin of Sinai. But this doesn't quite fit: it only usually occurs in the spring, can't be cooked in the way the Bible says, doesn't decay dramatically like the biblical manna, and even in a vintage louse year in the densest tamarisk groves, there's not much of it.

Breakfast for us is dough, more or less cooked in the embers of the acacia-wood fire, smeared with jam and onions. It gets tedious after a while. Food is just about the only sensual pleasure you have out there, and meals and the height of the sun are the primary markers of the day's passing, and so you obsess about it. Might it be sardines for lunch? Is there any of the egg-plant left? Just think what they'll be eating in the Windsor now…

And the Israelites had exactly the same food fantasies. 'If only we had meat to eat,' they said. 'We remember the fish we used to eat in Egypt for nothing; the cucumbers, the melons, the leeks, the onions and the garlic…there is nothing at all but this manna to look at.' 'Look at', note: not 'eat'. Those refugees knew very well that part of the pleasure of food is its anticipation. They were famously delighted when the wind gusted a cloud of exhausted quails into the camp from the sea. 'Meat,' they no doubt said, 'at last'.

I know how they felt. One of the great sensual experiences of my life was finding a forgotten can of corned beef at the bottom of a saddlebag after three weeks on bread and beans. It did me a lot more good than the quails did the Israelites. A plague devastated the people who had succumbed to the meat-lust, and they were buried in a place called Graves-of-Craving. I just got torrential diarrhoea.

After breakfast we break camp. It is an easy and quick business. We do not talk, but I am never sure why. The camels, gently complaining, are caught and saddled. Blankets are shaken and folded. The kit is put into flour-sacks and slung over the saddles. Water-bottles are filled. The fire is kicked out.

With Moses there would have been a great chattering and, if the Bible is right, often a great moaning. The children in modern Bedouin villages are eerily silent at night, but their volume rises with the sun. The Israelite children would have been the same, playing noisily and being scolded by their irritated grandparents. There would have been always a great urgency to pack up, because the camp would only be on the move if the cloud above the Tabernacle lifted and moved on. They wouldn't want to be left behind by God.

The only urgency for us comes from the great dictator: the sun. We want to make good progress before we feel it on the crowns of our heads. Chris is insane about the sun. He trots blithely along in a stained Def Leppard tee-shirt, grinning at his blistered forearms, wearing a *keffiyeh* of mine round his neck like a girl because he's left his hat on a bus. Every couple of miles I tell him a nasty story about sun-damaged DNA.

We always set off with a destination in mind. We know, more or less, where we will sweat out the real heat of the day, and under which pitted wall, rearing into the blue, we will pitch our camp that night. We follow roads of camel-dung and the prints of flip-flops that might have been there since the last rains, and I occasionally check the compass that swings around my neck, or ostentatiously hold a twig to my watch to check the direction by the sun.

But the Israelites marched by a cloud and a promise. In the night a fiery cloud hung over the Tabernacle. 'Whenever the cloud lifted from over the tent, then the Israelites would set out; and in the place where the cloud settled down, there the Israelites would camp... At the command of the Lord they would camp, and at the command of the Lord they would set out.' Perhaps the cloud shaded them from the sun. When the cloud went, the Ark went too, and the Ark would find their resting-place. And their long-term objective? They knew that Jahweh had promised them a land. It was a land not far away. For a lot of the time they were poised on its borders, peering lasciviously into it. But God seemed to be taking a very strange route to get there.

We walk alone, although in a strung-out pack. The desert finds you out, and reduces you to your lowest common denominator, and so to talk would seem like indecent spiritual exposure. Deep down, Chris is cheerful and sorted. But I know that I've been seen and known, and see terrible auguries in the gullies and the way the grass falls and the flickering eyes of the Rock Thrushes.

The real teaching sessions are the hot midday ones. There is an echoing dread when the camels are pulled down at eleven. I look round at the midday camp as a man who knows that he will hear a devastating prognosis views the doctor's door. Nothing can reach into the desolation of this time. I've tried all the strategies. It doesn't help to read P. G. Wodehouse: the gulf between his sunny world and mine just points up the isolation. It doesn't help to read the *Iliad*, because you are taunted by the distant surge of the Cannakale sea, and, after all, they were all there for something. It doesn't help to read the Bible, because, for all its privations, this place was a point on a journey for them: a journey with a confident if rather mysterious itinerary. My worry is that I'm not on a journey at all, or if I am, that I'm dramatically and dangerously off *piste*. And I daren't natter to Chris, because if that fails, then I really am at the end of the road. You should never test your last lifeline. When the demons really come cackling confidently around, licking their lips, it's important to know that there's one last blunt-nosed psychological round in the chamber. So I sit glowering in a cave, throwing stones at stones, and then lie down on my side and breathe in the rock-dust that was at the summit of the pinnacles when the Israelites passed by. And here comes the only comfort: Jerusalem smells of this hot rock too.

I watch the flies, wonder where they bred, and think that their complexity is wasted here. In my arrogance I used to think that my complexity was wasted here too. Now I know a very different story indeed.

There is real happiness when you hear stirring. The boy goes off to drag the camels away from the thorns. The old man stamps on the fire. Chris tells me where he's got to in the *Seven Pillars*, and says that Susie would hate eating quite so much okra in palm oil. And suddenly we're marching again, and everything is all right.

Those afternoon marches are pure joy. Your psyche is demob happy, the ravens display exuberantly for you in the high thermals, the geckos seem young instead of crushingly Jurassic, you are drafting passages in your head for the journal at the end of the day, the sun doesn't seem actively spiteful, there is cheese for supper and, most of all, there are the first whispers of the poetry of the night. The day is tediously, uncompromisingly prosaic. It's like a badly translated plumbing manual, and the cistern it refers to so brutally is your soul. The day seems bad, too; no doubt because of its most awesome sternness. The night is caressingly antiseptic.

Often, too, there are guests in the evening. The Bedouin are gregarious and conservative people, wedded to habits, routes and tea-drinking. And so, although Sinai is big and sparsely populated, anyone hanging onto the coat-tails of the Bedou will find wilderness mercifully elusive. Trust me: there are states of mind, quite easy to drop into, in which a shamefully discarded Coke can or the tracks of a jeep can be a comfort. It is even more helpful to be stared at disdainfully over the evening rice by a moustachioed chain-smoker in a grubby *jalabiya*. Their talk is little stuff: will so-and-so get a subsidy to root rocks out of his land? Have you heard what's happening to the price of mutton in Sharm al Sheikh? Why do Aston Villa wear white socks? Only once did I hear anything remotely metaphysical, and that was a brief debate about whether animals went to heaven. (They do, apparently.) The argument turned, not on Koranic niceties, but on whether or not Mustapha from Nuweiba was drunk when he saw a phantom goat trotting into a baker's.

The Israelites' fireside conversation was not so banal. Refugees are naturally earnest people, and uncertainty makes philosophers out of farmers. They talked about what God was doing. Why did he choose that route today? What on earth or in heaven is he going to do tomorrow? Is Moses a reliable mouthpiece? Is it really necessary for God to wield the rod quite as swingeingly as he does? Moses has told us that the delay in entering the Promised Land is because of our impatient disobedience: but is it really disobedient to want urgently what God has told us we were made for?

Such matters were for the late nights. In the early evening they moaned about the food, the sand in their eyes and the weather. There were few immediate excitements during the Sinai phase of the wanderings (which might have lasted the best part of the actual or notional forty years – most of it very possibly in a static camp). Certainly, in Sinai, there was little to say about other desert people. After Mount Sinai the Israelites kept bumping into people but not, it seems, in Sinai itself. Perhaps the Amalekites were so stung by their defeat at Rephidim that they steered clear of the Israelites. Perhaps they were simply too far away from wherever Israel was camped for further raiding to be feasible. But other unseen peoples no doubt obsessed the Israelites. Israelite spies had penetrated through the Negev to Hebron (something that the Israelis are still quite good at doing), and had come back with a vast, tantalizing cluster of grapes and a rather depressing report. The Promised Land is not empty – Israel will have to fight for it: '...The people who live in the land are strong, and the towns are fortified and very large... The Amalekites live in the Negev; the Hittites, Jebusites and Amorites live in the hill country, and the Canaanites live near the sea and along the Jordan.' Those names, and the scent of the grapes, infused Israelite dreams.

God's plan was evidently to gratify those dreams right away. But when Caleb jumps up on a rock, rallying the people to immediate invasion in a Henry V-like speech, the other spies lose their nerve and start muttering. 'The land is full of giants,' they say. 'We are like grasshoppers to them. The land will devour us.' And the mutterings take root in the minds of the people and spring up quickly to become fear and despair. The old longings for Egypt and for death return. Joshua tries to correct the malicious misinformation of the spineless spies, but it is hopeless. Moses faces a full-blown mutiny, and God is on the point of pulling out of the whole Israel project.

But Moses, in what seems to twenty-first-century eyes like a cynically cunning appeal to divine self-interest, persuades God that this is not a good idea: if God kills the Israelites, as he is threatening to do, the Egyptians and the Canaanites will think that the annihilation indicates a failure by Jahweh, the Israelites' tribal God. 'If you are as concerned about the honour of your name as I am,' Moses argues, 'you won't do this.' And God relents and forgives. But the forgiveness has a price. No Israelite, apart from the faithful Caleb and Joshua, will see the Promised Land. Faithlessness has consequences. And here's the thing: the price of faithlessness is to lose the very thing that you faithlessly feared you wouldn't get. There is a frighteningly logical irony at the heart of the divine will. The mutiny is seen off, and a new course is set. Since southern Judea is crawling with well-equipped troops, we must outflank them: set out for the wilderness by the way to the Re(e)d Sea. The geography at this stage is eye-crossingly difficult to reconstruct. Many different clandestine approaches to Hebron could fall happily within the Bible's account.

Around the spitting acacia campfires, presumptuous plans were hatched. God wasn't doing his bit. It was time for humans to take human matters into their own hands. There frankly didn't seem much to lose. God had told them that they weren't going to see the Promised Land, so they couldn't rely on him. The people launched their own invasion of the hill country of Judea. They had a curious battle cry: 'We will go up to the place that the Lord has promised,

for we have sinned.' Now that's odd. Perhaps they thought
that the Lord would help those who helped themselves. But
he didn't.

It was a disaster. 'They presumed to go up to the heights
of the hill country, even though the Ark of the Covenant of
the Lord, and Moses, had not left the camp.' They were
routed by the Amalekites, who chased them ignominiously as
far as Hormah (wherever that is). The people found that they
had a lot to lose after all. Their lives, notably; the prospect of
their children inheriting the Land; and a day-to-day relationship with the God who loved and fumed and remonstrated
and forgave from the Mercy Seat on the Ark of the Covenant.
Safety, both now and in the future, meant being where the
Ark was. At night it brooded in the heart of the camp; it had
killed for apparently minor ceremonial transgression; it had
planned the route; it seemed to be some sort of conduit to
the heavens; it hovered over the land, if you believe the later
rabbinic embellishments of the story, burning up thorns and
scorpions in the Israelites' path; it was terrible to have, but
more terrible not to have.

Chris scratched his badly scorched head. Laid out in front of
him on the sand was an air pilotage chart showing the Sinai
peninsula and surrounding lands, and a Bible, open at the
Book of Numbers. He was more confident with the map than
with the Bible. He had survived in the Scouts until he was
thirteen: he'd been thrown out of Sunday school at eight for
biting and blasphemy.

'Kadesh,' he said. 'Plainly the same as Kadesh Barnea. It
seems to be near somewhere volcanic or earthquake-ridden,
because just a few chapters before, three chaps get swallowed
by the earth. It's at the edge of Edom; they've got a water

problem, solved miraculously. And the Israelites seem to hang around there for some time. Also it seems that this was the last big stop before the push north: so perhaps they were there at least in the fortieth year.'

I had wondered if I'd missed something, and wanted his fresh eyes to look. But he had given a fair summary of all the available information about Kadesh. Yet to dispute the scholarly consensus that it is in eastern Sinai, at or near present-day Ain el Quiderat, is to invite buckets of academic phlegm. Well, I invite them. I reckon that Kadesh is more likely to be somewhere east of the Jordan river, somewhere in southern Jordan, and perhaps not all that far from Petra.

To get there I had to leave Chris and Egypt behind. I dumped Chris at the hottest gas station this side of hell, said that I'd see him in London, and felt awful. As my car shuddered off towards Taba, the last I saw of him was a very red hand waving at me and trying to point out his visa stamp to a hopeful policeman in search of *baksheesh*. Then the usual sullen chaos of Egyptian customs, the usual icy efficiency of Israeli security and the usual merry incompetence of Jordanian immigration.

CHAPTER 4
Toward the Sunrising

East of the Jordan, toward the sunrising…

Joshua 1:15

Whenever the Ark set out, Moses would say: 'Arise, O
Lord, let your enemies be scattered, and your foes flee
before you.' And whenever it came to rest, he would say,
'Return, O Lord of the ten thousand thousands of Israel.'

Numbers 10:35–36

W hen I got into Aqaba I dumped my kit, stood
under a cold shower for an hour and walked out
into the dusk. The air was like soup. I sat at a
table by the beach swatting mosquitoes, cats and children and
looked over towards Eilat, Aqaba's neighbouring Israeli non-
neighbour, which was just flickering into life. The border
between the two is a thin mined strip, a standard-of-living
discrepancy of about a thousand per cent and the accumu-
lated prejudices of people in suits and *jalabiyas* who have never
been to either place.

I feel kindly towards Jordan. Always have. Its people
make the cheerful, if rather listless best of its sand, grit and

rock. For millennia it has been, quite literally, a sideshow. No one came here because they wanted to come. They came because it was strategically necessary to be here (the Romans and the Crusaders), or because there was an economic vacuum that needed to be filled (the Nabateans), or because they couldn't live where they really wanted to (the Palestinians). This was the most penal posting, reserved for the naughtiest Roman soldiers or the most embarrassingly dissipate governors.

Aqaba is a hot, gentle town, full of giggling Saudis come to swig the liquor that would get them flogged and locked up half an hour away, to buy duty-free Cohiba cigars, and to splash merrily in the Red Sea. It's like a 1950s Broadstairs, but with burkhas.

I drank pomegranate juice, noted the Russian cargo ships sending their hopeful crews ashore for what they would find was a disappointingly chaste evening, heard an Israeli disco boat start to thump tediously up and down between Eilat and Taba, saw the mountains of Sinai ripple as the sun fell, and watched the swimmers trying to avoid the propellers of the glass-bottomed reef-boats. They're very enthusiastic but not very good swimmers, the Jordanians. I challenge you to spot a Jordanian swimming crawl. They're all earnest breast-strokers, and they hate to get their heads wet. So they stretch their heads painfully up, and puff and wheeze because they can't breathe properly like that, and then give up and wallow round in the shallows. It's impossible not to like them very much indeed.

They all swim an effortless crawl in Eilat, and never break sweat. Eilat is sleek and sassy. It undulates with improbably bronzed, improbably babe-ish babes, dazzlingly

oiled and wearing little except an assault rifle. Eilat is feline:
Aqaba's like a damp, romping dog.

Eilat/Aqaba (geographically it is ridiculous to divide
them) is the biblical Ezion-Geber. An intelligent child, looking at the map, could write its history from first principles.
Throughout recorded history it has been of pivotal importance. Here the Red Sea pushes a long finger north into the
desert of the Near East. From the southernmost tip of Sinai
you can sail almost half way to Jerusalem. And if you do, you
disembark at Ezion-Geber. Control Aqaba, as Lawrence
famously knew, and you control north-west Saudi Arabia.
For as long as anyone can tell, swaying caravans bringing
incense and spice from Yemen all passed through Ezion-
Geber and so, later, did pilgrims travelling between North
Africa and Mecca. It was in Aqaba that they would breathe,
wash, drink and commit themselves to God before stepping
into the haunted wastes of Midian or Sinai.

The Israelites passed through too. The Bible mentions it
only in a couple of lines, although on any view it must have
been a significant staging post. Wherever they were coming
from, Ezion-Geber was the first light on the home runway.
Moses had a clear flight plan. He wanted to go directly north
from here, along the King's Highway, which still runs
between Syria and Aqaba. Tourists going between Amman
and Petra tend to spend one cramped and emetic day travelling along it in their bald-tyred mini-buses, and another
going along the Desert Highway, an alternative route. Moses
had petitioned the King of Edom in the most conciliatory
way: '...let us pass through your land. We will not pass
through field or vineyard, or drink water from any well; we
will go along the King's Highway, not turning aside to the

right hand or to the left until we have passed through your territory.' No, said the King of Edom. And Moses meekly agreed, and decided to go around Edom. The problem for me is that it is not at all clear exactly where he went.

When I got back to my hotel there was a troupe of overweight, moustachioed soldiers in full desert gear plus Sam Browne bandoliers, jigging solemnly around to a very approximate 'Scotland the Brave'. As I said, it's impossible not to like this place.

Wherever Moses went from Ezion-Geber, it seems he went west of the ancient, arid kingdom of Edom, and eventually to the Zered valley. But that description is hardly helpful. It is often said that the Bible's description of Moses' dealings with Edom indicates that the Exodus account was written long after the events – probably in the seventh century BC – because it describes a powerful, coherent Edom that existed in the seventh century but didn't exist in the late Bronze Age. The people who say this haven't kept up with the archaeological journals. Recent work shows quite plainly that Edom existed and was copper-rich in the late Bronze Age; but even so, it was frankly a pretty shabby kingdom at the time. Edom was bounded by Ezion-Geber to the south and the Zered river to the north, which flows east out of the southern tip of the Dead Sea and spills to the east into the furnace of Arabia. Edom's western boundary, though, was amorphous. There were no Bronze Age Churchills drawing lines on the map in pencil after lunch and in barbed wire after dinner. All we can say is that it seems likely that at some stage the Children of Israel headed more or less north along the Wadi Arabah, and are unlikely to have gone east of the King's Highway until they crossed the Zered valley. They may have followed those mini-buses up the Desert Highway. And although it was getting dangerously near the forbidden territory, they might have gone near to or through Petra.

'We're in Kenya,' said Saleem, as we drove north from Aqaba through the Wadi Arabah. What he meant was that the acacias huddle together to form a canopy of whistling thorn, and the grass is like steel. But he was more fundamentally right than he knew. For the Arabah is the extension into the Near East of the Great African Rift. When man was born on the savannah of East Africa, he was, even as an infant, very restless. He started to walk. And one of his first big journeys was north along the Rift. It took him to Palestine, where some of the earliest fossils of osteologically modern man have been found. Because he walked along the Rift he never, in a sense, left Africa. There are other ways in which we as a species have never left it either.

As Moses and his people struggled up the Arabah they were reliving one of the most ancient human journeys, and in doing so were reinterpreting it for the world. The Arabah stretch of the Exodus is a crucial piece of exposition of the human story. Australian aborigines walk the land to make it dream, and the walking is the dreaming, and the dreaming is birth and redemption. For the Israelites things were slightly different. They said that redemption was found in the arrival, not the walk. But they also knew that re-enactment of the walk is central to proper arrival. You haven't really arrived in Jerusalem unless you continue to walk when you are there.

The Arabah has not changed since those first men used it as their bridge to Asia and Europe. At its northern edge it dives into the Dead Sea, and so it is nearer to the centre of the earth than anywhere else on the globe. It is white at noon, and lurching up at its sides, in Israel and Jordan respectively, are mountains that writhe with the changing light and cage the sun in the valley when dark comes. To the east the mountains rise to a vertiginous ridge that peers through mirage into Arabia. To the west is a more intimate desert, the Negev. In the Negev at night there is sometimes a whispering breath of blue air from the sea foam, for the whole of the western Negev is a beach. And in the north the pulse of Jerusalem begins to shudder through the sand.

Even in the southern Arabah there is a sense of homecoming. The Bible feels it. The pace in the Exodus accounts quickens as soon as the Israelites leave Ezion-Geber. The compass guiding the mission swings definitively north. There are some details to sort out, and there will be some episodes of dismal doubt, but the old promises suddenly start to solidify.

To drive up the Arabah is to drive up the seam between two worlds. To the west is Israel: to the east is Jordan. And what a lot is said in those simple statements. On the Jordanian side the border is a dead-flat pan of grit marked by pointless guard posts on stilts, each manned by one unfortunate soldier. The sentry boxes have no sides, so that if, under the crushing weight of the sun, the soldier dares to sit down while watching westward for the tanks of the Zionist aggressor, he'll be reported by the picnickers en route to the leafy niches of the highlands. On the Israeli side there are brave little greenhouses, and irrigation pumps thump away.

Arab tradition insists that the Israelites came through the Petra area before beginning the diversion around Edom. The Bible tells us that Aaron, the brother of Moses, whose rod was, in some accounts, lying alongside the tablets in the Ark of the Covenant, died and was buried at Mount Hor. Mount Hor, say the Arabs, is Jebel Harun, a blunt, waterless tor

looming over Petra. Nearby is Ain Musa – the Spring of
Moses – one of many places in the Near East where Moses
miraculously struck water from the rock with his staff, earn-
ing God's opprobrium for being too faithless merely to speak
it out.

Ain Musa today is a polite pool inside a mosque. Because
it has been adopted by the Muslims, the Christian tour
groups have decided that it is bogus, and it is mercifully left
to childless women and old men with gout. They bring their
sandwiches and make their healing into a proper day out.
When I walked in the women stopped their weeping and
started to giggle at my torn trousers.

Nobody ever forgets their first sight of Petra, and nobody
fails to record it breathlessly. That famous glimpse of the
Treasury from the echoing Siq needs no more adjectives from
me. This is a place whose august antiquity is immune to
everything that tourism can throw at it. It doesn't even
bother to sneer at the clicking Nikons, the panting, pop-
socked Nevada housewives, the bottles of coloured sand, the
lustful guides in tight trousers, the fake Nabatean coins, the
Korean-made plastic camels or the real reverence. It's a place
of terrible, implacable austerity, ringed by high places where
the priests killed unwilling victims to appease long-forgotten
gods.

The people who understand most about Petra's strangeness are Israeli. In the old, cold days of animosity between
Jordan and Israel, it was a rite of passage for adventurous
young Israeli men, often on their discharge from the army
and before they caught the plane to Kathmandu to find the
meaning of life, to take their Uzi and a water-bottle and set
out across the Arabah and up through the scented mountains

of Edom in search of Petra. They travelled at night, with the jackals. During the day they laid up in foxholes, as they had been taught, and God help them if they were caught, as they sometimes were. But if they weren't, they became high priests in a mystical Israeli aristocracy on their return to Tel Aviv, and never lost the bearing that came with it.

A few strides from the appointed path take you into a skeletal wilderness. 'Be careful,' said Saleem. 'They are primitive, these Bedouin. Even more primitive than donkeys.' He's a city boy in snakeskin shoes, and a commissioned officer in the old war between the desert and the sown; the pastoralist and the grower.

The Short-Tailed Ravens of Petra behave like eagles. I sat in a cave and watched them. Above the Monastery a tower of hot rock sends a plume of air spiralling into the sky, and they rode it like a roundabout as it bored upward. For an hour there was no wing-flap, and by then they were dots on the edge of the world. Then they saw that something had died in the north, and they folded their wings and fell like stones. From the top of their rise they would have seen all the remaining journey of the Ark before it got to the Promised Land.

There is an intense temptation to associate Petra with the Ark's journey. I share it. It is too good a site to waste. Some have placed Kadesh Barnea here; some have contended that Mount Sinai itself is one of the mountains around. The English writer Graham Phillips, for instance, thinks that the blue slate to be found here corresponds to the 'something like a pavement of sapphire stone' under the feet of God when he is seen on Mount Sinai by Moses, Aaron and many others in Exodus 24. And indeed he believes that the Ark was hidden here after its disappearance from Jerusalem. We meet his thesis later on.

Sitting in that cave, I wondered for the umpteenth time about what the Ark was, why it appears in the Bible story when it does, and (even more bafflingly) why it doesn't appear when you'd expect it to. In this Jordanian phase, just as in the Sinai and Wilderness of Zin phases, the Ark apparently navigates and chooses the camp. Presumably the Ark is at the centre of the Tabernacle as this gypsy God travels with his gypsy people. But although God is reassuringly prescriptive about the route and tells Moses that he will triumph over the enemies on the way, the Ark does none of the spectacular things that it does later on. It doesn't waste opposing armies, for example, although it would have been very convenient if it had. If, as is sometimes said, the Ark was a creature of Atlantean magic, and Moses was its controller, it seems that he hadn't learned at this stage to control it effectively. Whatever the Ark was, Moses was its servant, not its master. But the more I read this story, the less I understood. That's often the case with real stories and real people.

Moses had to push on north, and so did I. Saleem was getting restless for the bright lights of Amman and his wife's *baklava*, and I shared the Israelites' hunger for events, conclusion and greenness.

I was keen to get to Feinan, south of the Dead Sea and west of the King's Highway, which is widely thought to be the biblical Punon, and which, in turn, is thought by many to be where the brazen serpent incident took place. The Israelites, as usual, were whingeing about the food and the general misery of the place. They were slow learners. The whingeing was faithlessness, and faithlessness always made things much worse. On this occasion God sent a plague of poisonous snakes. Many Israelites died of snakebite.

We don't know what the snakes were. Later I went to the splendid Mizpe Ramon ecological centre in the Israeli Negev to view some candidates. I was introduced to them by an absurdly beautiful girl called Michal with short black hair, a PhD from Stanford and an impeccable war record in southern Lebanon.

'They might have been Field's Horned Vipers,' she said. 'They're very common. The problem is that the bite, although it produces swelling and bleeding, isn't fatal.' She sounded really disappointed. 'And they're very easy to avoid: they breathe loudly when they're approached, and you'd know they were there.'

I wasn't completely convinced by that. I stepped on one myself in the Sinai, and I was clumping around like an elephant. I was wearing thick boots, and it didn't hurt me, but the sight of a snake chewing at your foot can interfere with your evening.

'If you're looking for a really dangerous snake,' said Michal, happily, 'I'd recommend Burton's Carpet Viper. It bites like lightning, and often kills. Or there's this,' she went on, moving to the next cage, like a car salesman showing me the next model up. 'This is the Desert Cobra. It usually eats toads, and so it's often found near water, and so near human settlements. It's very venomous.' But there was a drawback, she said dutifully. 'It usually attacks with its mouth closed, and if it does bite, injection of venom takes several seconds.'

I looked at the notice on the cage. This slow injection, the notice solemnly assured me, gives the victim 'time to detach himself with relative ease'. I pointed to the notice.

'Relative ease?', I said. 'Is that a description given by victims?'

'Oh yes,' she assured me. 'You'll have no problem.'

I was impressed. If people in Israel prise cobra fangs out of their calves with relative ease, it explains why the country is so utterly invincible.

Anyway, the Israelites repented, and Moses interceded for them. 'Make a serpent and put it on a pole,' said God. And Moses did as he was told, and when anyone who had been bitten looked at the serpent, they lived. The Bible does not say where this incident took place, but Moses made the serpent out of bronze, and Punon was an ancient centre of copper mining. Hence, probably, the traditional association of Punon with the story.

Feinan (Punon) is a desolate place, and hard to find. It is trying very hard to rehabilitate itself, and has built an Eco-Lodge, to which we excitedly went. We parked under a corrugated iron shelter that you could have fried steak on. Even the flies were prostrate in the heat. The Eco-Lodge was an entirely empty room, bar some cycle racks at improbable places on the wall. There were no cycles. They're not stupid, these Jordanians.

An emaciated, immaculately white-robed man looked through us and poured out some tea in complete silence. We sat there staring at the piece of wall where there is usually a picture of the Kaaba in Mecca and of the King of Jordan looking calm in a dark suit.

Then the door burst open and the place erupted with khaki-shirted conservationists, mustard-keen to take us up to the copper mine and tell us why desert beetles are black (to give them a quick start in the morning so that they can get to the coveted dew) and that the Fat Sand Rat tended to get diabetes in captivity. Nobody came to this lodge, and all this information, laboriously acquired in Amman, had no outlet. We couldn't stem the flow:

'I can show you the burrow of the Golden Spiny Mouse,' said one.

'They eat mostly snails,' burst in another, elbowing his way past.

'The Dabb lizard,' insisted yet another. 'Now there's an interesting animal. It's vegetarian, which is unusual for a lizard, and it changes colour in response to the heat. In the morning it is dark —'

'Like the beetles,' the first conservationist reminded me.

'— and later in the day it is lighter,' continued the lizard man, shooting the beetle man a murderous glance.

Behind the lodge a wall of chameleon rock jumps into the undulating air and starts the land's climb towards Arabia. It is pierced by passes which are negotiable with a steady nerve, but where on earth is the water? The Israelites couldn't have carried much, and they weren't always smiting it from rocks along the way. Feinan town is a dusty clutter of breeze-block huts, alternately listless and watchful, losing its battle against apathy and the sand of the Arabah. It has been economically irrelevant for the past three thousand years. Behind the present town is the steep-humped Tel of ancient Punon. Nobody knew whether it had been excavated, and nobody cared.

By the time the Israelites got to Punon they had either gained sufficient confidence to thumb their national nose at the King of Edom, or they had already wound their way round his domain. In any event, it looks from the various itineraries as if they cut north-east to rejoin the King's

Highway. They stayed more or less on the Highway until they veered west for the final approach to the Jordan river. They crossed the Zered river at Iye-Abarim, which took them out of Edomite territory into Moab.

As soon as the Israelites cross the Zered, the tone of the biblical accounts changes. The Israelites always had proverbially stiff necks: now they get stiff martial backs. The music in the background had been tentative, complex and poignant. Now there's something of the Prussian brass band. And the geography itself is in crescendo. From now on they are on a rising ridge, with a vertiginous view to or sense of the western Dead Sea and the eastern Sand Sea. Every step takes you to a new spying post. Often there is a swirling curtain of dust to the east; often there is a black maritime pall to the west and even, once, gulls riding the clouds from Crete and dropping to squabble over the guts of a cat killed by a car outside a Roman temple to Jupiter.

I sat sweating happily from the Zered to the Arnon, looking westward. A cushion of haze sat over the Dead Sea, splintering the falling sun. The hills were like white lino at lunchtime: now they were shivering velvet, and cloud shadows crawled over them like vast deformed animals.

The Arnon valley is the most spectacular wadi in the Middle East. An astonishing serpentine road, taking the course of the original King's Highway, winds up and down. This is the most tortured and exposed of landscapes. You can see every storm and every trickle of the last 30 million years. The natural contours are terraced by ancient goat paths. When the Israelites got here they knew, if they had not realized before, that God was painting the story of their salvation on a very big canvas indeed. Suddenly, too, you feel a long way from Egypt. Exodus is a serious business.

A Bedouin man squatted in a lay-by. Fossils from the valley were laid out on a *keffiyeh* and he was drinking Sunny Delight from a tin mug. He had sold five ammonites this year. This was October. He slept in an old grave high up in the valley wall, had a Grey Shrike in a cage, and was reading John Le Carré in Portuguese.

There were troubles ahead, but this time the Israelites didn't go quietly. Sihon, King of the Amorites, whose seat was at Heshbon, refused them passage, as the King of Edom had done. Their response? When Sihon's army came out to bar their way, 'Israel put him to the sword, and took possession of his land from the Arnon to the Jabbok, as far as to the Ammonites…their posterity perished from Heshbon to Dibon, and we laid waste until fire spread to Medeba.' This is language we will hear many times in the history that follows. It was the first of many genocidal victories for the Israelites. They apparently did it without the express intervention of the Ark, although not, they'd no doubt say, without the intervention of the God of the Ark. He was certainly thanked by the warriors when they wiped the Amorite gore off their swords.

Modern Dhiban is the biblical Dibon-Gad, the Moabite capital. It was feted in biblical times for its succulent pastures. It was the sort of place where a Levantine Amaryllis would be serenaded in rhyming couplets. It is long grazed out now. It's a purely Bedouin area, although lots of the ethnic Bedouin live in shacks built over running sewers. When you walk through the town the children only bother to wipe the flies from their eyes so that they can see where to throw the stones.

'I need to go to the Tel,' I told Saleem.

'It's over there,' he said, waving his arm vaguely. 'They're very violent near there. They'll trash the car.'

'I need photos,' I insisted. 'Ahmed will keep watch.'

'We're not insured for places like this,' he replied, stiffly.

I leapt onto my high horse and out of the car. 'I'll walk.'

Saleem sat on the bumper bar and watched me stride off.

One hour and a lot of bemused expressions later, I returned. Nobody knew where the Tel was.

'I'm not surprised,' said Saleem. 'It's nowhere near here.'

We drove frostily north.

Although the pace of the story gathers quickly once the Israelites press past the southern tip of the Dead Sea, there are some intriguing suggestions that they might have stayed around in Moab and Ammon for quite a while: '...Israel settled in all the towns of the Amorites, in Heshbon and in all its villages... Thus Israel settled in the land of the Amorites...and took possession of [the land of King Og of Bashan]', we're told. And 'while Israel was staying at Shittim, the men began to have sexual relations with the women of Moab. These invited the people to the sacrifices of their gods, and the people ate and bowed down to their gods. Thus Israel yoked itself to the Baal of Peor...'

It is a picture not of the invariable brothel visits of any passing army, but of slow assimilation and consequent compromise. Maybe that is how it was. Perhaps Moses was poised for years on the very edge of the Promised Land, not as an embattled refugee but as a successful warlord, consolidating

his hold on the region from a stone-walled fortress in van-
quished Heshbon.

The Tel of ancient Heshbon has a well-preserved Roman
temple on top. Modern Hasban is an affluent city with lots of
grotesquely ornate houses with views of other ornate houses.
Its mosques are tidy and theologically moderate; its olive
groves are small and neat; its prickly pears are middle class.
'It's a nice place,' said Saleem, checking his cufflinks. 'Lots of
the best building contractors in Amman live here.' I could
well believe it. On the Tel a blackstart hopped from an Iron
Age shard to a Roman shard.

'Beware of judging a city by the size of its Tel,' they told
me in Israel. I was also wary of judging this one by the size of
its biblical reputation. You could walk round this Tel in two
minutes, even if you were badly disabled. 'Come on,' shouted
Saleem from the car. He had not wanted to scuff his shoes on
those shards. 'There's nothing here.' And he was right. But
there had been something very big indeed. If the Bible is
right, it seems that it was here that the Jews had their first
intoxicating taste of sovereignty. This was the first proper
Jewish-ruled town in history. There were to be many more.

When the Israelites moved west for the final push, they
camped in the mountains of Abarim, in front of Mount
Nebo. There, Moses reminded them of everything that God
had done for them. And then one of the Bible's most moving
scenes was enacted. God had told Moses that he would not
cross over the Jordan himself. Moses was a hundred and
twenty years old (or three notional forty-year generations,
which might not be at all the same thing). 'Ascend the mountain,' God told him. 'You will die there and be gathered to

your fathers. Although you may view the land from a distance, you shall not enter it...'

So Moses went up, and God showed him the whole land: Gilead as far as Dan, all Napthali, the land of Ephraim and Manasseh, all the land of Judah as far as the western sea, the Negev and the Jordan valley as far as Zoar. Although it is a magnificent panorama, it is not quite that good. Josephus, writing in the *Antiquities*, notes that it 'affords a view of much of the excellent land of Canaan.' Much indeed, but not all. As later rabbinic commentators pointed out, Moses would indeed have needed God's help for such a view.

Mount Nebo is the summit of Mount Pisgah, which was one of the notorious High Places of Moab, drenched with the propitiatory blood of human sacrificial victims. Moses was another victim on that High Place, but his death instituted a new type of salvation. He died there, and his mantle passed to Joshua, who was to take the Land. Moses was buried in a valley in the land of Moab opposite Beth-Peor, says the Bible, 'but no one knows his burial place to this day.'

That's an interesting and significant line. Moses was a leader of supreme importance, and yet his grave was unmarked. That would have been unthinkable in Egypt, with its magnificent cult of death. If the Israelites saw life and death as the Egyptians did, they would have built Moses a pyramid of gold. But they were no longer in Egypt. Judaism celebrates life; it does not glory in death. The laws of *kashrut* and the prohibition on intermarriage had set them apart from the nations, but this was far more fundamental. The Israelites were high priests of a cult of life.

Mount Nebo is an amorphous mountain, but its stature grows as you approach it. So does its complexity. It looks from a distance like a gently folded lump of speckled clay, but it gets nuance as you get closer. The road exposes the complexity: it starts to curve and then meander, and then to throw itself about as it curls around the wadis. There's a church on the top with some of the most exuberant zoological mosaics the Byzantines ever did, and a monument whose theology is diplomatically ambiguous. They are all very well, these Jordanian Christian shrines, but for me they're devotionally inert. Who would choose to live here and tend them? The whole point of Nebo is that it is supposed to be behind you.

Nebo stands more or less opposite Jericho. The Israelites marched from Nebo to Abel-Shittim. And there, in the sweltering plains of Moab, Joshua got his invasion instructions from God. Perhaps he was on his face before the Ark, hearing the voice from between the cherubim. The instructions were geographically explicit and utterly ruthless. Their gist was: This is my land. I am giving it to you. There must be no compromise with the inhabitants. The policy is straightforward ethnic cleansing. If it is not done thoroughly there will be a terrible price to pay: '…[I]f you do not drive out the inhabitants of the land from before you, then those whom you let remain shall be as barbs in your eyes and thorns in your sides; they shall trouble you in the land where you are settling. And I will do to you as I thought to do to them.' When, later, the Israelites' genocidal zeal flagged, God was indeed displeased, and urged them to more complete compliance.

In Abel-Shittim the Israelites got a stiff lesson about compromise and assimilation. We have seen how they went off with Moabite women, and so went off with Moabite gods.

Jahweh was fiercely angry, and the penalty was a devastating plague.

Militarily Abel-Shittim was a good place from which to launch a campaign. It is now Tel Hammam, and is literally a minute from the Allenby Bridge, the central crossing-point between Jordan and Israel. The Tel rises high above the police station in a ragged village living off Allenby bureaucracy and bananas watered by the Jordan river. Everything droops here. All the green is tangled. The only deep shade is in the courtyards of the subdued mosques, and from the bananas. The aeons visibly interlock in the shards on the Tel. 'This is late Bronze,' says Saleem, kicking the base of a beaker. 'And that' (pointing to a jug handle sticking out of a half-hearted excavation) 'is Iron II.' The white noon light sucks all the colour out of the land. The acacias throw a lace-work pattern over the roads. Everything in the village is unfinished. In every pool of half shade there's an old woman in black. Mount Nebo rises mistily to the south-east, and all the cars throw up a pillar of cloud. A boy with a *keffiyeh* held in place by a baseball cap chases some sheep into a thorn-bush stockade.

The target is clearly visible across the valley: Jericho, the city of palms. When the warm wind gusts from the west at night, it sometimes brings the scent of parsimmon – the palm balsam so precious in the ancient world.

'Be strong and very courageous,' God told Joshua on the eve of the invasion. 'Do not be frightened or dismayed, for the Lord your God is with you wherever you go.' And he was. The Israelites set out from Abel-Shittim and camped for three days by the Jordan. It can sometimes seem that long when you are crossing the tedious checkpoint at the Allenby

Bridge. It is one of the many grand farces of Middle Eastern politics. Jordan doesn't stamp you out: you are only going into the West Bank, after all, and if you're Jordanian, the West Bank is part of Jordan. But as you cross into the Israeli-controlled area, you are taken apart, very politely and apologetically, by the bored Israelis who have drawn the short straw of service at the Bridge. If you're a Jordanian wanting to cross into the West Bank, don't bother.

On the night before the invasion, Joshua told the people to sanctify themselves. 'Tomorrow the Lord will do wonders.' 'Follow the Ark', he said, 'but don't follow it too closely. There must be about a kilometre between you and the Ark. The priests will carry it on their shoulders.' It was the time of harvest, when the Jordan was in full, dangerous flood. It seemed impassable. But when the feet of the priests touched the water of the Jordan, an astonishing thing happened. 'The waters flowing from above stood still, rising up in a single heap far off at Adam, the city that is beside Zarethan, while those flowing toward the sea of the Arabah, the Dead Sea, were wholly cut off.' This has happened occasionally since. In 1266 a big landslide at Adam cut off the Jordan. This isn't to deny the miraculous nature of the event. If this happened as the Bible says, it was a true miracle of timing.

Then the people crossed to the other side. 'While all Israel were crossing over on dry ground the priests who bore the Ark of the Covenant of the Lord stood on dry ground in the middle of the Jordan, until the entire nation finished crossing over the Jordan.' The Ark, or the God of the Ark, had started the final march well in the vanguard, as the Ark had always done since Sinai. And the Ark, or the God of the

Ark, was the last to enter the Promised Land. God was watching the Israelites' backs too.

CHAPTER 5

Conquest

Now proceed to cross the Jordan, you and all this people,
into the land that I am giving to them, to the Israelites...
No one will be able to stand against you all the days of
your life. As I was with Moses, so I will be with you; I
will not fail you or forsake you. Be strong and courageous; for you shall put this people in possession of the
land that I swore to their ancestors to give them...

Joshua 1:2, 5–6

With the crossing to the Promised Land, the Ark,
which has been out of the text for a while, is suddenly in every other line. It seems as if it is glad
to be home too. The first thing Joshua did when he got to the
west bank of the Jordan was to remember what Jahweh had
done. He ordered twelve men, one from each tribe, to take
a stone from the river-bed and lay them down in the camp.
They were later set up in Gilgal, 'so that all the peoples of the
earth may know that the hand of the Lord is mighty, and so
that you may fear the Lord your God for ever.' There was
apparently another set of stones set up by Joshua in the middle of the Jordan where the priests' feet had stood. 'They are

there to this day', says the Book of Joshua. Neither they nor the stones at Gilgal have ever been found.

Nobody has ever found Gilgal, either, although Vendyl Jones, whom we will meet later, insists that he has. I must have seen it, though, dozens of times. It probably lies somewhere east of Jericho, just off the road that carries to the Bridge minibuses of wedding guests in their best suits, film crews with steel briefcases and flak-jackets, and juggernauts taking blocks of Hebron stone to front the big houses in Amman. It's a desolate, white, cracked land between two oases, criss-crossed by jackal tracks. But in Joshua's day it wouldn't have been such a wilderness. The Jordan has shrunk to a trickle since then, siphoned off for green peppers in plastic hothouses and for the thirsty cisterns of Israel, and starved at its source by Turkey's and Syria's incontinent demands for baths.

This time I walked alone along the road towards the biblical baptism site, watched by a lot of anxious binoculars. A family of desert partridge exploded at my feet and went cackling off over the border. I sat in a ravine, kicking the mud from a flood about ten thousand years ago, and turning over in my hands an earthenware fragment that might have been early Bronze Age. Jericho itself has been continuously occupied for longer than any other known place on this earth. On this trip I spent a lot of time doing things like this, frustrated at the alternate exhibitionism and elusiveness of the long dead.

Joshua camped at Gilgal, hacked off the foreskins of the uncircumcised with flint knives so that they would be consecrated holy warriors, waited for the wounds to heal so that they could run without pain, and spied out Jericho. The people of Jericho had no doubt heard about the martial prowess of the Israelites against Moab, Ammon and Bashan. They saw what was coming, and sealed the city. It did them no good.

For six days they stood on their battlements watching a strange procession. The Ark of the Covenant, preceded by seven priests blowing seven ram-horn trumpets, circled the city, along with all the warriors of Israel. Whatever else it may have been, it was devastating psychological warfare. Nemesis came on the seventh day. On that day the procession started again, but this time there were seven circuits of the city. On the seventh circuit Joshua cried out to the people: 'Shout!' They shouted, and the trumpets blew, and the wall, ancient even then, fell flat. They charged into the city, sparing only the family of Rahab the harlot, who had harboured Israel's spies.

At Jericho the Ark was no secret weapon. The secret weapon was the God of the Ark, in his accustomed place in the middle of his people. But no doubt rumours began to spread of the powerful box that could flatten walls and kill thousands.

Joshua's collision with Jericho means a collision, too, between the archaeological consensus and the Bible's account. Quite simply, the dates don't seem to work. The traditional date for the Exodus from Egypt was around 1440 BC – a date calculated mainly from 1 Kings 6:1, which says that Solomon's Temple was built in the 480th year after the Exodus. The Temple was built about 960 BC; 480 years before that is 1440 BC. Proponents of this date point to the rule of the foreign Hyksos over Egypt, which ended around 1550 BC. This could be, they say, the time of Joseph's prominence in Egypt. The king of the Exodus, 'who knew not Joseph', might then have been the king at the time of the expulsion of the Hyksos, and the oppression of the Hebrews might be Egyptian retribution on the now fallen foreigners who had long had the upper hand. The case for this early date seemed clinched when, in the 1930s, John Garstang excavated Jericho and found an impressive destruction level that he dated to 1400 BC. It was perfect. Departure from Egypt in 1440; the Conquest in 1400, after the biblical forty years of wandering; and here were the remnants of the wall that Joshua's trumpets so famously sent tumbling. The Bible was triumphantly vindicated. Sceptics trembled.

But Garstang had got it embarrassingly wrong. Kathleen Kenyon's meticulous re-excavation of Jericho in the 1950s showed that Garstang's destruction layer dated to around 1560 BC – in the Middle Bronze Age. This was only the final nail in the coffin of the early date. Albright, in the 1930s, had demonstrated destruction levels that he dated to around 1250–1200 BC in several Palestinian sites, and had correlated them with the appearance, particularly in the highlands, of a distinctive new people. If these incomers were the Israelites, this would make Rameses II the Pharaoh of the Exodus, and made sense of some details in the biblical account of the flight from Egypt which were difficult to square with the earlier date. Albright put the Exodus at around 1290 BC and the Conquest at 1250–1200 BC.

Today only a few conservative diehards cling to the early date. There are no mainstream archaeologists amongst them. In fact the archaeological improbability of the early date need not mean that the Bible is wrong: 480 years is 12 notional generations of 40 years – which is how generations were conventionally but optimistically reckoned. Mortality being what it was in those days, a generation was likely to be less than 40 years. The overwhelming consensus is that if the

Exodus and the Conquest happened, the Exodus is a late Bronze Age event and the Conquest an early Iron Age event. But many have difficulties with the notion of 'events'. Many see the Exodus as a gradual drift, probably of many different groups, or even as the mounting influence of a group that had long been seeded in Palestine.

Although the late date consensus holds, Albright himself has taken a battering, and Jericho remains a headache for those fundamentalists who have been able to stomach the late date. Kenyon decided that the relevant bit of Jericho was destroyed in about 1300 BC. If the Bible really did mean that Rameses II was the Pharaoh of the Exodus, this was too early.

And there the argument has stuck. But it is not as worrying for the scriptural conservatives as it is sometimes said to be. Jericho has been pretty comprehensively shredded by armies, earthquakes, weather and archaeologists. Reading its strata is notoriously difficult, even with the help of modern scientific tools. Further evaluation is complicated by Molotov cocktails and masked men with Kalashnikovs. I am no biblical archaeologist, but I have learned what a very fluid science archaeology is. The unimpeachable dogma of today becomes the laughable banality of tomorrow. The intellectual landscape changes perceptibly with every edition of the journals. I can think of no more exciting academic rollercoaster, but you don't tend to get terribly accurate bearings from the back of a roller-coaster.

The best approach to Jericho is from the Jerusalem–Jericho road, down the Wadi Kelt, past the desert monastery of St George, and out into the Jordan valley past the Mount of Temptation. I used to walk it on my own about once a fortnight with a bottle of water, a bag of oranges and battered copies of the Bible and the Koran. I used to lie up happily in the worst of the heat, watch the stream when it was there, and see what the sun did to the rock. If I know anything at all about how time moves and how old the world is, I learned it there. When I got to Jericho I ate hummus with the Bible propped up in front of me, picked my way uncomprehendingly over the excavations, and caught a shuddering, belching bus back to East Jerusalem. Now they cut your throat in the Wadi Kelt.

Jericho has seen some splendid palaces. When the Jerusalem winter crept into Jewish, Greek and Roman bones, their owners crept off to Jericho, where you never need more than a shirt. The most prominent building in modern Jericho is the casino – the only major building that Yasser Arafat ever built. It has failed dismally, of course. The oil squillionaires of the Gulf choose to waste their riyals in Dubai and Monte Carlo rather than poor beleaguered Palestine.

I slung my bags into a shared *servees* taxi in Jericho, paid for three places so that we could get going more quickly, and started the ascent to Jerusalem. We will come back to Jerusalem. The Ark, of course, didn't make it there for hundreds of years. It is enough to say that however many times I make the journey to Jerusalem, it is a journey of ecstasy. The excitement at the first sight of the first rooftops is the real thing, which cuts through all cynicism, all attempts at detachment, all scepticism, all contempt for fanaticism. Jerusalem turns philosophers into fanatics and raises the dead. Jerusalem is the beginning and the end of the road. It's what it's all about.

Just off the Jericho–Jerusalem road is Nebi Musa – the burial-place of Moses, according to Islam. It's a desolate place at the end of a bad road. There's nothing there but a mosque, a tired man slumped in a deckchair fingering his worry-beads, and a glorious view over the mountains of Judea. Its significance is obvious. Islam wants to claim Moses and take control of his story. It's not in the nature of Islam not to know things. Islam wasn't happy with the Deuteronomy story of an unknown resting-place for this towering prophet. Nebi Musa is part of an Islamic marketing strategy which fits theologically very well with the rest of the faith. We can complete the story, it says. You needn't muddle on with half truths any more.

I set up base camp in a dusty, empty and dour Arab hotel in the middle of a screaming *souk* in the Old City of Jerusalem. In the early mornings I ate cheese on the roof, heard repeatedly from the only other guest how easy it was to stow away in the water-tanks of boats crossing to Finland from Tallinn, and read about the parasites recovered from the Essene toilets in Qumran. And then, at eight o'clock, I trotted through all the aromatic chaos of the Old City (where I have been happier than anywhere in the world), to start my days with Lee Glassman.

Lee came to Israel as a highly successful American businessman and stayed to become a highly successful human being. He's as jaunty as a Covent Garden barrow-boy, his Hebrew's dreadful, he's obsessively neat (I bet his underpants have knife-edge creases), he's got a strong Pennsylvanian accent, a heavily annotated Tanakh, an encyclopaedic knowledge of Israel, and when he sees red tape he's like a rabid dog with enhanced cunning. He's about the best company on the planet.

I climbed into his immaculate car at the Jaffa Gate, rip-

ping some of the flags from his maps and soiling his seats with
a plum I'd sat on that morning. 'You breakfasted?', he asked,
mopping the seat with a wet-wipe. 'Then let's go to Bandit
Country.'

After Joshua's victory at Ai (during which the Ark seems to
have been left back in camp in the Jordan valley), Joshua
renewed in the Promised Land the Covenant with Jahweh
that Moses had made. He built an altar on Mount Ebal of
unhewn stone, and made, probably on some stone pillars, a
copy of the law of Moses. The Ark was central to what happened next:

> All Israel, alien as well as citizen, with their elders and
> officers and their judges, stood on opposite sides of the
> Ark in front of the Levitical priests who carried the Ark
> of the Covenant of the Lord, half of them in front of
> Mount Gerizim [the Mount of Blessing] and half of them
> in front of Mount Ebal [the Mount of Cursing]…and…he
> read all the words of the law, blessings and curses, accord-
> ing to all that is written in the book of the law…

Simply verbal affirmation of the Covenant does not seem to
have been enough. God himself had to be there to witness it
and to participate again in the contract. Hence the Ark. It is
an important place. And not just to Jews. Gerizim is the holy
mountain of the Samaritan sect. They believe it was here that
Abraham prepared to sacrifice Isaac.

But it is not easy to get to. It is high up in the hill country of Samaria, just next to Nablus (the biblical Shechem),
which is an epicentre of Palestinian violence. En route from
Jerusalem we picked up a couple of people who knew the
area and could read its political moods. First there was Esti

Herskowitz, a vibrant New Yorker with a Talmudist's systematism and a Kiplingesque gift of clear and colourful expository story-telling. And then there was Jabo, officially, but seldom, known as Ze'ev Erlich. Jabo was an old Samaria hand, built for ploughing, as happy in a library as in an armoured car, and as unselfconscious as a toddler.

We drove first to Jabo's house in the settlement of Ofra to pick up some supplies and some recent military intelligence. In his garden there was a field gun used in the 1948 War of Independence, some milk cans labelled with the Hebrew names of villages destroyed in that war, and the skulls of some local mammals. We drank water, ate some rusks, and looked at the rows of books written by his ancestors. 'He should have stuck to philosophy, that one,' said Jabo, indicating books as if they were tombstones, which in many ways they were. 'His imagination was pulverized by gunfire, and his novels are unreadable.'

We drove north, into the most verdant hills of the Occupied Territories. A lot of work has gone into these hills. They are heavily terraced, and divided up with little drystone walls. Their very sophisticated irrigation systems might go back to Israelite times, and the great-boled olive trees might easily have seen Jesus.

We stopped to eat at an Israeli army canteen where the various burger and hotdog options had the names of military units. You could have a Paratrooper with fries, a Golani with extra gherkin or a Givati with coleslaw. Young soldiers, both male and female, slouched happily around, drinking Coke and smoking Marlboro Lights. It was difficult to remember that this was a serious business. 'Every week the Army here catches a young boy who wants to blow himself up on a bus in Israel,' said Jabo. 'Every week. You don't hear it on the news. It's not news. It's normal.'

We wound cautiously up to Mount Gerizim. Nablus was below, and away from it, on all sides, rolled the hot, fecund hills of a barbarous Tuscany. We could have thrown a stone into the refugee camp where a lot of the dissent breeds. Shots rang out, but nobody bothered to do anything. In Mandatory times the British, bless them, planted trees on Gerizim (because it was blessed), but not on Ebal (because it was cursed). We don't know where the Ark was. It may have been on the site of Nablus itself.

In Nablus lie the ruins of Joseph's Tomb, a site sacred to Jews. It was destroyed by Palestinian activists, and Ehud Barak decided to reduce political temperatures in the town by pulling out the Israeli soldiers who were guarding the tomb. He won few friends on either side for doing so. Jews are barred from Nablus now. Some of the regular worshippers at the tomb decamped to a nearby settlement, Yitzhar, high on a barren ridge, clearly selected as a place that could be held by a few men against many. It now holds about 150 families. Many of the boys are called Yusef. The name 'Yitzhar' means 'the first drop of oil squeezed from the olive'. Everything is a slogan in this land.

When we drove up to Yitzhar, the whole place stank of smoke, and the grass on one of the slopes was blackened. A couple of nights before, local Arabs had tried to burn the place down, but the alarm was raised, the families in the most precarious homes evacuated, and the fire put out. It was nothing worth commenting on. 'It's how we live,' said the hugely black-bearded Yigal, who lived in the settlement. 'Some people watch baseball. Some people take the dog

round the park. We snatch our children from the flames and
hit the gas if we see a roadblock. It will be this way until
Mashiach comes.'

Yitzhar is the repository for some of the artefacts sal-
vaged from the ruins of Joseph's Tomb. Some have remarkable stories. In the synagogue at Yitzhar is a
sixteenth-century silver ornament from the top of a Torah
scroll. It had been looted from the Tomb by Arabs in the
nineteenth century, and sold to a tourist. It had passed into
the great maw of the Holocaust, been vomited out in East
Germany after the war, recognized and returned to the
Tomb.

I have long since concluded that, for an outsider, the only
arguable position on the Israeli–Palestinian question is confused agnosticism. The more I see, the less I know. Perhaps
you can't get into the heart of the Exodus before seeing the
hot despair of a Palestinian refugee camp. But I'm certain of
this: if you don't like what they're doing at Yitzhar, you
wouldn't be able to bear a moment of Joshua's company.

After the renewal of the Covenant at Mounts Ebal and
Gerizim, Joshua strode through the land with terrible single-
mindedness, winning some famous victories. Most of the
stories have a chilling litany: '…he utterly destroyed every
person in it; he left no one remaining'; '…he struck it with
the edge of the sword, and every person in it…'; 'Joshua
struck him and his people, leaving him no survivors…';
'…every person in it he utterly destroyed that day…' There
was enmity with everyone, and this was Jahweh's doing. The
Bible is quite explicit:

> There was not a town that made peace with the Israelites,
> except the Hivites, the inhabitants of Gibeon [who had
> brokered a treaty by trickery]; all were taken in battle.
> For it was the Lord's doing to harden their hearts so that
> they would come against Israel in battle, in order that they
> might be utterly destroyed, and might receive no mercy,
> but be exterminated, just as the Lord had commanded
> Moses...

But there were limits to Joshua's martial energy. Some parts of the land remained unconquered. They were to be debilitating thorns in the Israelites' side.

The mopping up continued for some time, but when the Israelites' hold on the land was consolidated, the cultic base-camp was shifted from Gilgal to somewhere more central: 'The whole congregation of the Israelites assembled at Shiloh, and set up the tent of meeting there. The land lay subdued before them.'

But is that really how it was? Did the Israelite confederation really emerge out of the wilderness in cloud and fire? Was the land won in a flash of bloodied bronze swords?

Avi Faust is Professor of Archaeology at Bar Ilan University, and probably knows more than anyone about the evidence for the emergence of a distinctively Israelite people. I wanted to speak to him because in his writings he seemed able to stay off his hobby horses. Biblical archaeology is deafeningly full of preachers with megaphones on soapboxes. But he seemed sufficiently humble and confident to articulate the consensus. We met in a restaurant in downtown Jerusalem. I bought him tofu and apple juice and scribbled away in my notebook.

I suggested that the Merneptah stele had to be the starting point for every historian wanting to trace the genesis of the Israelite nation. Faust agreed.

In 1896 Flinders Petrie, who was excavating the mortuary temple of the Pharaoh Merneptah at Thebes, discovered a black granite slab. The slab has on it a poem, in hieroglyphs, commemorating the Pharaoh's campaign in Canaan in 1207 BC. 'Canaan is plundered with every evil; Ashkelon is conquered; Gezer is seized; Yanoam is made non-existent.' And then the line that took everyone's breath away: 'Israel is laid waste, his seed is no more.' This plainly overstated the case, but it was monumentally important. By 1207 BC there was a national entity in Canaan that called itself Israel and was sufficiently significant to be worth adding as a notch on the Pharaoh's victory belt. Merneptah was the son of Rameses II. If Rameses was the Pharaoh of the Exodus, the pace of Israelite nation-building had been impressively quick. Too impressively quick for some commentators.

It fits, said Faust, with what you see in the ground. 'If we had no Bible and no stele, archaeologists would start talking about a race distinct from the Canaanites sometime in the thirteenth century BC – from around 1200.' It is then that you see the explosive emergence of a completely new society.

Canaanite communities in the late Bronze Age had gone demographically downhill since their earlier halcyon days, probably because of Egyptian depredation. They slowly recovered, and by the end of the era most of the Canaanite population was concentrated in big, central settlements. These were towns, not villages, usually from 30 to 100 dunams in area (a dunam is 1,000 square metres), but up to 600 dunams in some cases (Hatzor). The population of each was a few thousand. The jury is out as to whether they were properly walled cities. It seems that politically Canaan at this time was a conglomeration of city-states. The more numerous lowland cities had relatively smaller territories; the fewer highland cities had bigger territories. They were all subordinate to Egypt. The succession might have been formally hereditary, but all rulers ruled only so long as Pharaoh smiled on them. Egypt, at least until the twelfth century BC, maintained garrison towns in Gaza, Jaffa and Beit Shean to enforce obedience in general and tax payments in particular. The Tell Amarna tablets record some tale-telling to the Egyptian schoolmaster by one Canaanite city-state against another. 'They're not paying what they should pay,' was the gist. They were surprisingly cosmopolitan people, these Canaanites, with trading connections across the eastern Mediterranean. Mycenaean and Cypriot imports are found in practically every site of the period. But most of the trade was domestic: they swapped agricultural surpluses. And their economic independence was strictly limited by the heavy Egyptian yoke. Canaanite slaves did a lot of the Egyptian dirty work around the region. Manpower was always a problem. It is suggested that some of the wars between city-states were slave-seizing forays.

If the Bible is right, this was the culture that Joshua destroyed. The obvious question, though, is why the Egyptians would stand for it. There is no mention in the Bible of any Egyptian sorties against the Israelites. The Merneptah stele suggests that the Egyptians did not tolerate whatever the fledgling Israel did, but clearly Israel did survive. Perhaps Merneptah was cautious of messing with Israel. If the Red Sea crossing narrative has any truth in it, his

father's army was destroyed by the vengeful God of these turbulent Israelites. Or perhaps the explanation lies in the geography of the Conquest. Perhaps the Israelites were saved
precisely because they didn't conquer all the land that they
had been told to conquer. For most of the military successes
that the Bible records in detail were in the highlands. And
Egypt wasn't very interested in the highlands.

The brand-new society that burst into existence in the
thirteenth century was in the highlands. During the late
Bronze Age there were few settlements there. The ones that
there were, were big cities by contemporary standards. Then
suddenly, in the Iron I period, the map of the highlands is
spattered by hundreds of new, small settlements. They are
not only new; they are different from anything that existed
before in the region. The Canaanites of the late Bronze Age
experimented with decorated pottery, and imported a good
deal of pottery too. The new, Spartan people of the highlands
had no such ceramic fripperies. The Canaanites had quite
elaborate cave-burials, which often gave away the status of
the body. The incomers had simple, unfussy inhumations.
Their dead were equal. The Canaanites had temples: the
incomers had cult places, but no temples. Who were these
incomers? 'Well, here's the thing,' said Faust. 'They didn't
eat pigs.'

The concordance between the biblical account of the
Conquest and the archaeological consensus is, therefore, a
rather approximate one. But, again, it's not as rough as it has
sometimes been painted. And some of the main criticisms of
the biblical account seem to me to be misconceived. It's said,
for instance, that there is no evidence of the destruction, at
the material times, of a lot of the towns said to have been

devastated by Joshua. That's unfair. It's based on a misreading of the text. Joshua's general policy seems to have been to 'take' the towns, not to destroy them. There are only three cities that the Bible clearly says were destroyed. The first was Jericho: we have dealt with that already. The second was Ai. There are tremendous difficulties in identifying Ai. The commonest identification is with Khirbet-et-Tell, but it is so dubious that nothing firm can be concluded from the non-evidence of destruction. The third is Hazor, and there there is indeed evidence of destruction by fire at approximately the right time.

CHAPTER 6
Consolidation and Captivity

There is no Holy One like the Lord, no one besides you;
there is no Rock like our God.

1 Samuel 2:2 (the Song of Hannah)

We practise alchemy in reverse – touch gold and it turns
into lead...

Aldous Huxley, *The Genius and The Goddess*

'When you're dealing with Middle Eastern archaeology, Middle Eastern politics, theology, life in general and Shilo in particular,' said Jabo, 'the most important word, and by far the most difficult word, is "maybe".' We were looking down from the modern, heavily guarded settlement of Shilo, in Samaria, onto the likely site of the first long-term resting-place of the Ark of the Covenant.

The most impressive thing about the site is how unimpressive it is. The mound of the Tabernacle is overshadowed by high places with splendid views. Almost anywhere else would have made more obvious sense. It must have been chosen for precisely that reason. Probably the Jahwehists were deliberately dissociating the seat of their God from the Canaanite high places. Perhaps this was simply to avoid confusion and therefore assimilation. No Canaanite god would ever be worshipped in a valley. Or perhaps it was a theological statement of great confidence in their God. Perhaps it was saying that their God's power did not depend on where he was put. Indeed, he wasn't a God who could be put anywhere at all. He was the greatest, and therefore putting him in the lowliest physical position wouldn't affect his potency in the slightest. At the Tabernacle in Shilo irony and paradox entered the world's theological lexicon.

Two adjacent sites on the low mound have been suggested as the position of the Tabernacle. Here, archaeology is simple speculation, and it doesn't matter much who is right. We don't know, either, exactly what stood there for all those years. The Bible simply says it was the Tent of Meeting – the mobile sanctuary used during the wanderings. Later comments attributed to God record him saying that 'I have not lived in a house since the day I brought out Israel…I have lived in a tent and a tabernacle…' The Mishnah, however, insists that there was a roofless stone structure covered by the Tent. Inside, arranged and adored according to the instructions given in Sinai, was the Ark of the Covenant itself.

At the foot of Tel Shilo are a Byzantine church and a mosque. Both were probably built where the builders thought the Tabernacle stood, in a blatant attempt to say that their faiths encompassed, superseded and corrected the older faith of Judaism. But the builders got their archaeology wrong. The church and the mosque stand near where the city gates must have been. There's an ancient almond grove there. 'It sprang from the rod of Aaron,' said Jabo. 'Maybe.'

Scorching political temperatures have put Shilo out of bounds for most Jewish people. It is a tragedy. The connection with the dawn of Israelite national history is better attested and more movingly tangible here than anywhere else. It's the sort of place that makes mystics out of orthodontists. If Alan Garner were a Levantine Jew, he'd have set *Red Shift* here.

When Joshua knew that death was pressing close, he gathered all the tribes to Shechem. There, 'the elders, the heads, the judges and the officers of Israel...presented themselves before God...' This presumably means before the Ark, although the Ark is not specifically mentioned. If that's right, then the Ark was merely based customarily at Shilo, but could be moved about for special events. We don't know if the Tabernacle went with it on its wanderings, but it would have been difficult to comply with the detailed stipulations of Sinai if it did not. There's a suggestion, though, that the Israelites gradually got ceremonially sloppy. David, when he moved the Ark towards Jerusalem, simply slung it on the back of an ox-cart. Aaron would have been horrified.

Just like Moses did before his final departure, Joshua reminded the Israelites what Jahweh had done for them, and, inspired by the recollection, the people reaffirmed their part of the Covenant. But they and their descendants turned out to have short memories. After all of Joshua's generation was gathered to their ancestors, 'another generation grew up...who did not know the Lord or the work that he had done for Israel...'

And so we move into the era of the Judges. It's a messy part of Israelite history, characterized by the periodic unfaithfulness and repentance of Israel. The pattern is depressingly repetitive. The faithlessness is shown by failing to complete the Conquest and by running off after the gods and the women of the remaining inhabitants of Canaan. The faithlessness of incomplete genocide makes possible the faithlessness of intermarriage and apostasy. Complete political and spiritual annihilation is averted by heroic 'Judges' – men and women parachuted in by Jahweh to save the day. But they are themselves of uneven obedience and spirituality. There is lots of epic, colourful stuff, and lots of real danger for Israel, but only one word about the Ark, which one might think might have been usefully deployed at crisis moments. When we meet it again it has been moved yet again from its base camp in Shilo. This time it is in Bethel, just north of Ramallah (or Mizpah, not so far away from Bethel), and the army is in despair at its failure in a civil war against the tribe of Benjamin. Jahweh's counsel is sought. It is interesting that it is assumed that to enquire of God is to enquire of the Ark:

> ...the Israelites inquired of the Lord (for the Ark of the Covenant of God was [at Bethel] in those days, and Phinehas son of Eleazar, son of Aaron, ministered before it in those days), saying: 'Shall we go out once more to battle against our kinsfolk the Benjaminites, or shall we desist?' The Lord answered, 'Go up, for tomorrow I will give them into your hand.'

So of course they do, and of course God does.

But these are sideshows in the story of the Ark. The service before the Ark at Shilo, conducted by a cadre of trained professional priests had, with a few interruptions, been faithfully continuing. The aura of cultic sanctity that you see as soon as you open 1 Samuel was no doubt the norm throughout the previous years too. But the priesthood had started to go bad. The rot was most evident in Hophni and Phinehas, sons of Eli, Jahweh's priest at Shilo. They treated with contempt offerings made by the Israelites to Jahweh. Normally they would have succeeded their father to the priesthood, but Jahweh had other plans. He would not be served by corrupt men. The way he chose to get the Ark out of their hands was an extreme and dramatic one.

Lee met me early in the morning. There was a lot to do that day. We drove out of the Jaffa Gate, through the waking suburbs of Jerusalem, and out onto the main road towards Tel Aviv. We drove past the soldiers on their way back to their bases after the weekend, past the black-coated ultra-orthodox waiting for the bus to the Western Wall, past the new cemetery, dug because Jerusalem is such an internationally popular place to die in, past the monastic winery of Latrun, past the ruins of the vehicles knocked out in 1948 as they were trying to lift the Arab siege of Jerusalem, through deep cuttings lined with cypresses as straight as pencils and out into the flat and fertile coastal plain. There we turned north towards Petah Tikva, the first major settlement of the Zionists and now a big and unattractive satellite in the Tel Aviv conurbation.

The site we were after was mighty elusive. We drove round and round and up and down in the nightmarish rush-hour traffic, shouting 'There!' and 'Surely they couldn't have meant that', and reversing suicidally into fast-moving lanes. Eventually we saw what might have been a Tel rising above the road, skidded to a halt on the hard shoulder, put the emergency lights on and climbed over the barriers up to the top.

Across the road a massive grey wall of some industrial plant blocked the view to the sea. On our side the respectable, red-roofed houses of office workers gradually gave way to fruit farms and vines. Pylons strode across the land. At the top of the Tel we kicked around in the dense, dry grass and found a fallen sign. We turned it over. In faded Hebrew it told us that we were at Ebenezer.

When Eli was an old man a vast Philistine army marched against Israel. The armies encamped within a couple of miles of each other. The Philistines were at Aphek; the Israelites at Ebenezer, which is on the ridge looking down towards Aphek. In the first clash Israel was routed and took heavy losses. The situation was critical. The Israelite commanders held an urgent conference at Ebenezer: 'Why has the Lord put us to rout today before the Philistines? Let us bring the Ark of the Covenant of the Lord here from Shilo, so that he may come among us and save us from the power of our enemies.' The theological reasoning is hard to follow. God is capable, from wherever he is, of determining the course of the battle: hence the Israelite losses. But if the Ark is brought, God will in some particular sense 'come among us' and his will, when the Ark is there, will be different (more pro-Israelite) than it was before.

The Ark was duly brought from Shilo, and as it was carried into the camp the Israelites raised their great battle roar. Today it would be drowned by the grumble of the motorway or soaked up by the white tower blocks and their smoked-glass windows. The Philistines discovered what the roar meant, and they thought they were doomed. The reputation

of the Ark had spread, but they too were theologically confused. 'Gods have come into the camp,' they said. The
Israelites were plainly failing to get the monotheistic message
across.

'Woe to us!' wailed the Philistines. 'For nothing like this
has happened before. Woe to us! Who can deliver us from
the power of these mighty gods? These are the gods who
struck the Egyptians with every sort of plague in the wilderness.'

But they rallied and fought. And a strange thing happened. Not only was Israel defeated, but the Ark of the
Covenant was captured and its keepers, the sons of Eli, were
killed.

This little Tel of Ebenezer, part of the wasteland of Rosh
Ha'Ayin, a dump for suburban hedge-clippings, tyres and
nappies, was a turning-point for the Jewish people. The
Israelites had called expressly on Jahweh's Ark to help them
in a pivotal battle. Throughout the Exodus the Ark had
meant military success. But now the battle was lost and God
himself was in the hands of the enemy. The world suddenly
seemed upside down. Things weren't simple any more.
Doubt was injected deep into Jewish history and psychology.
It has been there ever since.

Back in Shilo, Eli sat by the road, waiting and watching.
He had never wanted to let the Ark go, and he was fearful for
it. If his old eyes had been up to it, he could have seen from
a long way off the approach of the ragged Benjaminite who
had run from the battlefield, his clothes torn and the earth of
mourning on his head. But he was blind, and the messenger
had to be brought to him. The Benjaminite told the catastrophic news about his sons and the Ark. The news of the

sons was bearable; the news of the Ark was not. Eli fell backwards off his seat and snapped his neck.

Phinehas' wife was propelled into premature labour by the news. The child's name was Ichabod, which means 'the glory has departed from Israel'.

But God was playing a long game. The ecstatic victory feast of the Philistines proved to be pure poison.

They bore the Ark off to Ashdod. We followed it, through a green, sedate land pocked by outcrops of wildly tilted white rock, past regimented lines of fruit trees and telegraph poles, each with its own turtle dove. 'Even the toilets of this country are romantic,' said Lee. 'There's the pumping station built by the British after their conquest of the Turks. It pumps all of Jerusalem's water. Until it was built, Jerusalem was supplied using the basic plumbing installed by King Herod.' Off the main road, dark ravines filled with singing conifers burrowed into the hill.

The modern town of Ashdod is an island of whitewashed towers in a sea of dunes. To the east are Israel's main transport arteries, throbbing away in a corridor of fruit. To the north children play on a hill called Givat Yonah – the hill of Jonah. Jewish and Muslim traditions agree that Jonah was vomited by the great fish onto the beach here, and that from here he began his missionary trek to Nineveh. The sea is tired. Today's wind started in the hills of Sicily. The masts of little boats swing like pendulums, counting time until the precisely prophesied end of the age.

Spectacular though a lot of them are, the Philistine Tels of Israel are an esoteric taste. Exact information is hard to come by. That was why we looped off to pick up Silvie Neuman, who works for the Israel Antiquities Authority and spends a lot of her life digging up Philistine cities and illustrating their artefacts. She was proudly proprietorial about Tel Ashdod. 'It doesn't look much from a distance,' she said, 'but there's no doubt at all about the attribution, and skiploads of important Philistine stuff have been found here.' The obscurity of the place is a testament to the extraordinary archaeological richness of Israel. Anywhere else, a site this important would have its own visitor centre selling Taiwanese tat and earnest, badly translated guidebooks, and there'd be a roped route and brass notices giving long-rejected archaeological conclusions. But in Israel, where they have more than 30,000 known sites – and where everywhere, really, is a site – they have to pick and choose what they throw money at. So Tel Ashdod, where Dagon's Temple stood, was excavated, written up, and then buried again.

To get there you squeeze through a broken gate and wade through waist-high grass and resentful cows to the summit. To the west a long line of breaking surf points to the glowering bulk of Gaza. Ominous plumes of black smoke drift inland from Gaza City. To the east, there is a sizzling hiss of sprinklers on the most fecund soil of the Middle East, and, far beyond, the blue haze over the Judean hills. None of the Philistine town is above ground. The Tel is topped by a derelict Ottoman house and this, more or less, is where the Temple would have stood.

Dagon was an ancient Syro-Palestinian god who had been enthusiastically adopted by the Philistines. The Ark of the Covenant, borne in triumph back to Ashdod, was placed beside his image in the Temple. It was plain that the Israelite god was subject to Dagon; Dagon had won the day. But the Ark was still powerful and to be revered. With both the Ark and Dagon on their side, the Philistines would be formidable indeed.

But the God of Israel was not a tame god. When the people of Ashdod went into the Temple early the next morning, Dagon was prostrate before the Ark. It was hardly auspicious, but they picked Dagon up, dusted him off and put him back on his pedestal. The incident was an embarrassment, but what happened next was a disaster. The following morning they found that Dagon had again fallen flat on his face before the Ark, but this time his head and both his hands had broken off. The meaning could not be plainer. Contrary to the message of the battlefield, Dagon was subject to Jahweh, and impotent beside him.

If this had been all that happened, the Philistines might simply have swapped Dagon-worship for Ark-worship. But that was not what Jahweh had in mind. To have God in the right place means blessing; to have God in the wrong place means cursing. And curse he did.

The curse in Ashdod meant an epidemic of some 'tumour'-producing disease – very possibly bubonic plague, which generates big nodal swellings. Later on in the account it seems that it was associated too with an epidemic of mice, which may have been vectors of the disease. The people of Ashdod were in no doubt about the connection between the disease and the Ark: 'The Ark of the God of Israel must not remain with us; for his hand is heavy on us and on our god Dagon.' They convened a conference of the Philistines, and the people of Gath, for some reason, volunteered to take the Ark.

Perhaps it was bravado. Perhaps it was a bit of spiritual one-upmanship, designed to show the people of Ashdod that the priests of Gath were more able to keep this troublesome Israelite god on a tight rein. And no doubt it was unthinkable, at this stage, to send the Ark back to Israel. It would have been like rearming your worst enemy after you had just neutralized him. But, anyway, the Ark went to Gath. And so, of course, did we.

This is where a lot of what the world knows about the Philistines has been found. Silvie digs here a lot, and there was no containing her as we drove there. 'This is where Goliath was from – you know that, don't you? There's no need to dig anywhere in Israel but here: we've got it all, from Iron I, or earlier, to the Ottomans. You'll see how compact and well coordinated the Philistine world was: you can signal all the other Philistine towns from the top of Tel es-Safi. Excavating here's amazing: imagine sharing your barbecue with all those Iron Age ghosts. They're far better company than most live people.'

Tel es-Safi (Tel Gath) is in a sort of hot, Levantine Buckinghamshire without foxhounds. The approach is through a quiet little forest park commemorating Israeli war dead. The Israelis do these things well, and rightly put children's playgrounds on the top of their monuments, which shows that they've understood quite a lot about quite a lot.

It is massive: far and away the most visually impressive of the Philistine Tels; big enough for different moods and diversions on the way up. One of its folds was a piece of cliché Peloponnesian Arcady; hanging bowers and happy sheep all set to panpipes. But it soon gave way to the stern strategic realities: a sweeping command of the land in every direction – 360 degrees of natural battlements, the top ones enhanced by perching on the bones of their predecessors.

'Here's the tidiest and most productive square of all,' said Silvie, showing us up to her patch, neatly sandbagged against the winter rains. She knew the successive inhabitants of that small square, from the Iron Age onwards, as intimate friends. She shared a lot with them: the friendly and terrible sun on the wings of the Gaza gulls; the Aegean squalls spiralling down to break in thunder on Jerusalem; the problem of where to get water, and where to defecate.

'I'm happier with the Bible when it talks about the Philistine campaigns,' Faust had said. And most people are. There is broad agreement that the Bible paints a reliable picture of Philistine life.

By the time the Ark was seized the Philistines had been established in the coastal strip for 120 to 150 years. They lived in big, crowded, walled cities with impressive public buildings, and although their sites are littered with highly decorated pottery of Aegean origin and they are thought of as the quintessential mariners of the Eastern Mediterranean, they were surprisingly stay-at-home, agricultural people. Ambitious ships might occasionally have gone up to Sidon or over to Cyprus with a hold full of iron knives, but mostly they crawled up and down the Palestinian coast, and for every shekel made in international trade, a thousand were made by bartering wool and pomegranates with their Philistine neighbours in Ashdod, Ekron, Ashkelon and Gaza.

The Ark did dreadful things in Gath. 'The hand of the Lord was against the city, causing a very great panic; he struck the inhabitants of the city, both young and old, so that tumours broke out on them.' Again, it sounds like bubonic plague. If Gath had thought that its gods would trump Jahweh, they were sorely mistaken. They decided to get rid of the Ark, and this time it seems that they did not consult with the recipient. That was wise. Frankly, it wasn't much of an offer. Perhaps Gath was the senior partner in the Philistine confederation, and Ekron couldn't refuse. Anyway, to Ekron it went.

There was no archaeological intuition involved in the siting of Kibbutz Revadim. The founding fathers just thought it was a good place to grow cotton and oranges. The kibbutzniks worked the land for quite a time without realizing that there was anything here. And then they began to wonder whether the shards in every spadeful of the hot soil meant anything. They did: entirely accidentally they had built their kibbutz on the top of the ancient city of Ekron, lost for millennia.

'Now this,' said Silvie, shovelling down the eggplant salad in the kibbutz dining room, was a 'huge, huge, huge, huge city. It's the biggest Iron Age site in Israel. And if Gath really could push Ekron around, Gath must really have been the kingpin.'

From the kibbutz it's twenty minutes bumping along a dirt road to the Tel. You pass through a cloud of eucalyptus in a valley where the air's like treacle, and then out into the cotton. And there, more of a wrinkle than a mound, is the Tel. In Ekron you hear the voice of Ozymandias more audibly and more plaintively than anywhere else on this journey. No one comes here. Even the kibbutz workers were fuzzy about where it was. The rough grass that covers the Tel is not littered with the usual corroding Coke cans that say that an occasional school party comes here to be talked at. Thorns divide the huge stone blocks.

'It's difficult to feel even historical animosity against a people so comprehensively destroyed,' said Lee.

'I'm glad to hear it,' said Silvie. 'These are my friends.'

The Ekronites were scared stiff by the arrival of the Ark. Interestingly, they seemed to be more theologically informed than the Philistine soldiers at the battle of Ebenezer/Aphek. 'Why have they brought around to us the Ark of the God of Israel to kill us and our people?' It was a fair question. It was not a very brotherly thing for the Gathites to do, and the outcome was depressingly predictable. 'There was a deathly panic throughout the whole city. The hand of God was very heavy there; those who did not die were stricken with tumours, and the cry of the city went up to heaven.'

Yet another Philistine pow-wow was arranged, and this time the view of the priests and diviners was conclusive. They seemed less clear than the laypeople about the connection between the Ark and the catastrophes that had afflicted the Philistines. But there was a way to test the connection. A new cart was yoked to two milking cows, unbroken to the yoke, with calves at heel. In the cart was the Ark of the Covenant. The calves were taken away. The natural instinct of the cows would be to turn back towards their calves. 'But,' said the diviners, 'if some supernatural force overrides that instinct, and the cows head towards Israelite territory, then we will know that Jahweh really is behind our troubles. It would be dangerous, though, to send the Ark back alone. If Jahweh has sent this plague, he sent it because he was angry: he has to be appeased. Let's learn from the lesson of the unfortunate Pharaoh of the Exodus.' 'Some sort of guilt offering is necessary, they reasoned. It needs to be valuable, and what better than gold? And it needs to relate symbolically to the catastrophe, so that Jahweh can see that we are repenting sufficiently specifically for specific forgiveness to be possible.'

So they made five gold tumours and five gold mice, 'according to the number of the lords of the Philistines; for the same plague was upon all of you and upon your lords.' The gold tumours and the gold mice were put in a box alongside the Ark, and so began, somewhere on that low mound among the cotton and the oranges, the audacious experiment to probe inside the mind of God.

There must have been a big crowd out to watch it. And they must have been divided into two camps. Some must have wanted the cows to look for their calves. That would have meant that the Israelite god had no power to touch them, which might, in the long term, be the best thing for the Philistines. And it would have left untarnished the reputation of their own gods. Others, terrified by the plague, must have hoped devoutly to see the cows heading for Judea, carrying with them the source of the devastation and the hope of a cure.

There was no holding the cows. They went straight towards Beth Shemesh in Judea, 'along one highway, lowing as they went; they turned neither to the right nor to the left.' Later rabbis said that the cows burst into song as they pulled God along. Following them, no doubt anxious to make sure that they really were rid of the Ark, and no doubt curious about the reception that the Ark would get from the Israelites, came the Philistine lords. When they came to the Beth Shemesh border, they halted and watched.

'It's a nice bit of real estate, this,' said Lee. And it was. 'Very popular with the orthodox professionals. The doctors and the lawyers with the black *kippot* and the Subaru. Good for Jerusalem; good for Tel Aviv. Nice people, nice schools. And just enough of a teenage drug culture to make them feel that they're not missing out completely on the real world.'

We were standing on the ancient Tel of Beth Shemesh, looking down on the new town, which wasn't quite so intelligently situated. It's big, this Tel, and has been very diligently investigated. On the huge walls of dressed stone, crickets chirred in the fading light, hunted by wheatears, and a sparrowhawk on a swaying cypress looked lustfully at the wheatears.

Faust had dug here for about seven years, and was worryingly agnostic about it. 'Was it Israelite at all?' I asked, slightly irritated, after he'd spooned a big dose of caveats over the falafel. 'Well,' he said, 'probably, but not obviously.' Most would not share his caution. It is fairly well established that this was an Israelite settlement of probably 30 to 40 dunams, settled pretty densely, and smaller and much less impressive than its Philistine neighbours. No public buildings of any kind have been found in any Iron Age I Israelite towns, and Beth Shemesh is no exception. They did some trade with the Philistines who were intermittently their enemies: the few splashes of ceramic colour and pattern in the sandy strata of Beth Shemesh are probably Philistine. But their economy was overwhelmingly agricultural: they herded their sheep and goats among the shrub oak and cypress that covered the land in those days, and they grew hay and cereals.

Indeed, it was harvest time in Beth Shemesh when the Ark arrived. The reapers looked up and saw a very strange sight. They must have rubbed their eyes. There, in the back of the cart, was the Ark of God. It had been missing for seven months. We have no account of the Israelite mood during those seven months, but it takes little imagination to work it out. God was not dead: it was worse than that. He had either defected to the enemy or been shown to be an impotent vassal of their gods. The theology so grandly proclaimed at Sinai was in tatters. And so was the national identity that rested on it. Either God wasn't omnipotent, as he had insisted he was, or he wasn't passionately concerned with Israel, as he had said he was. Or both. But suddenly, because an ox-cart had appeared over the brow of a hill, the world was very different. The cart bore more than a box with some stone tablets: it bore a whole restored theology. It was possible still to be Jewish, as that had been defined at Sinai.

The cart rolled into a field and stopped by a large stone. The cows never did get to see their calves: the stone became an altar, and they became a burnt offering. The Philistines, watching from the border, were satisfied that the Ark would not be returning to plague them. They turned round and went back to Ekron. Had they stayed, they might have got some schadenfreudic pleasure.

For the rejoicing of the people of Beth Shemesh did not last long. The Ark proved too hot for them to handle too. Exactly what happened is not clear. One version says that the descendants of Jeconiah did not rejoice with the others, and that God killed seventy of them for their joylessness. Another version, in the Masoretic text, says that God was angered by people looking in the Ark, and that he responded with great slaughter. This would be on all fours with the draconian injunction in the Book of Numbers to the Kohathites, who served in the Tabernacle: '...the Kohathites must not go in to look on the holy things even for a moment', God stipulated, 'otherwise they will die.'

Whatever happened, it had the same effect in Beth Shemesh as it had had in the Philistine cities. The people of Beth Shemesh were desperate to get rid of the Ark. 'Who is able to stand before the Lord, this holy God?' they said. 'To whom shall he go so that we may be rid of him?' The expression, 'Who is able to stand...?' is an intriguing one. It has priestly overtones. The Beth Shemesh-ites might have been acknowledging that they did not have in their community a priest sufficiently skilled or experienced to deal with something as potent as the Ark, and that it needed to be referred to a more specialist centre. They referred, in any event, to Kiriath-Jearim, which is the modern Abu Ghosh. There's no Tel there, reeking of antiquity: just a cheerful, slightly dog-eared town on one side of a wooded ravine on the outskirts of Jerusalem, selling first-rate hummus and shwarma and apocalyptically dreadful fake bacon rolls.

It's maintaining a brave face despite the recent contortions of Arab–Israeli politics, but Abu Ghosh used to be a happier place. Its history is of sunny, mutually beneficial coexistence with its Jewish neighbours. The signs in the restaurants are in Hebrew; the restauranteurs' sons wear denim jackets and want to study marketing in Haifa; it was a popular place for Jewish Jerusalemites to pass an evening. And some still go. But it is changing fast. Many in the region hate happiness, and translate 'coexistence' as 'collaboration'. Poison is seeping into the schools from Jenin and Gaza. What affects the schools today affects the cafes, the balance sheets and the cemeteries tomorrow.

'The Ark was happy enough here, but slightly restless,'

Artist's impression of the Tabernacle during the Wanderings. The Ark is behind the curtain in the deep dark of the tent.

The charnel house of St. Catherine's Monastery, at the foot of Jebel Musa (the traditional Mount Sinai).

The start of the day: A camel bellows at the sun.

A sandstone skull leers out of a cliff face on one of those interminable afternoons.

The end of the day: Unpacking the camels and preparing to brew up.

The wastes of south central Sinai.

From one world to another: Looking back across the Red Sea from a rocking boat in the harbour of Aqaba, Jordan, towards the Israeli port of Eilat.

Camels wander up the desolate Wadi Hrava (Arabah), in Jordan – the extension into the Near East of the Great African Rift Valley.

The road snakes down towards the River Arnon, Jordan – the historic boundary between the Moabites and the Amorites.

The Moabite capital, Dibon-Gad – modern Dhiban.

The tel of ancient Heshbon – arguably the first Jewish-ruled town ever.

Looking westwards from the summit of Mount Nebo. To the left is the Dead Sea. It was from Mount Nebo that Moses got his glimpse of the Promised Land. He was buried at an unknown place on the mountain, and some think that the Ark of the Covenant is hidden on the mountain too.

Joshua's last view of the Promised Land before the invasion began. The view from Tel Hammam, Jordan, across the Jordan Valley to Jericho.

Over the Jordan. Near Gilgal, with Jericho straight ahead. In the distance are the mountains of Judea.

Looking down onto Jericho and the Jordan Valley from the Judean desert.

Looking from Mount Gerizim (the Mount of Blessing) to Mount Ebal (the Mount of Cursing). The modern Arab town of Nablus (Biblical Shechem) lies in the valley.

A politically inflammable refugee camp in Nablus, from Mount Gerizim.

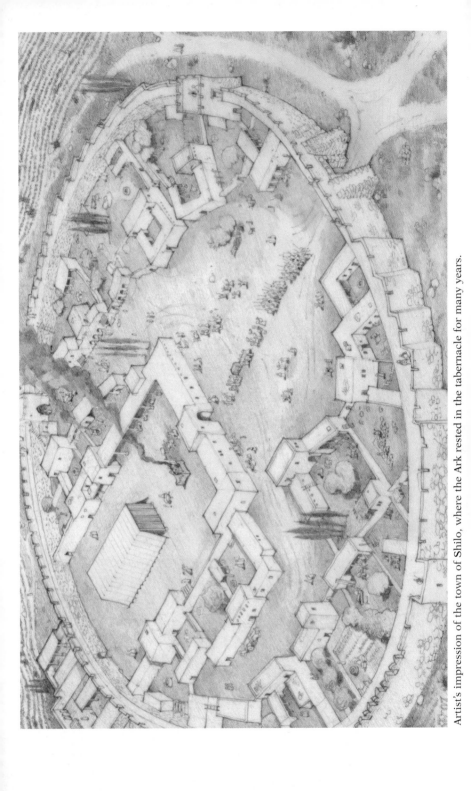

Artist's impression of the town of Shilo, where the Ark rested in the tabernacle for many years.

The lowly site of ancient Shilo, overshadowed by the surrounding hills.

Tel Shilo: looking up from near the probable location of the Shilo tabernacle

Modern tower blocks rise over the site of Ebenezer, the site of the Israelite camp during the disastrous campaign in which the Philistines seized the Ark.

The forgotten tel of Ashdod, where Dagon's temple stood, where Dagon's idol fell prostrate before the Ark, and where the Philistines first experienced the curses that travelled with the Ark.

The view from Tel-es-Safi, the Philistine city of Gath, where the Ark was for a while.

Old and new Beth Shemesh. Here the cows hauling the Ark back to Judea stopped. There was great rejoicing amongst the Israelites. But not for long.

Looking down from the City of David, Jerusalem, to the Arab village of Silwan (Siloam). Before the Temple was built the Ark was kept in the City of David.

A cut-away view of Solomon's Temple in Jerusalem, showing the Ark in the Holy of Holies, between the cherubim.

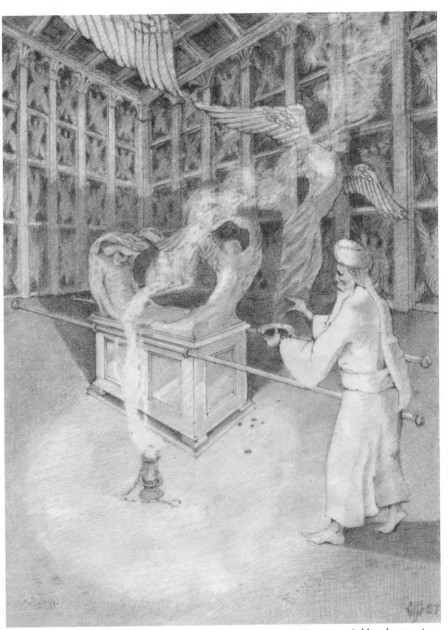

Swathed in white robes and incense, the High Priest on Yom Kippur sprinkles the atoning blood on the mercy seat – the lid of the Ark.

In the Western Wall tunnels, Jerusalem: The sealed door leading under the Temple Mount. If the Ark is where the Mishnah says it is, this is as close as you can get without starting World War III.

The highlands of Ethiopia, where many think that the Ark is to be found.

An Ethiopian priest at the Holy city of Lalibela, hewn from the rock by (depending on your point of view), angels, a sophisticated African civilisation, or the Knights Templar who had gone to Ethiopia in search of the Ark.

The Hill of Tara, Ireland. From the Mound of the Hostages (where some say the Ark is now concealed), to the Rath of the Synods where, in the 19th century, 'British Israelites' excavated in hope of finding the Ark.

The site of the ancient Warwickshire well where many think the Ark is to be found.

said Lee, spilling orange juice down one of those immaculate tee-shirts as we sat looking back over the terraced hillsides through which the Ark plodded up to Kiriath-Jearim. 'It could smell Jerusalem, just over the hill. But it was biding its time, and was being served properly for the first time in a while.'

That was a fair summary. The people of Kiriath-Jearim, undaunted by the fate of Jeconiah's descendants, came to collect the Ark. They took it to the house of Abinadab, which was on the hill, probably near where we were sitting, and consecrated Abinadab's son, Eleazar, to have charge of the Ark. Twenty years passed. They were eventful ones for Israel.

There was one more thing to see in Abu Ghosh. It was a significant thing. We got there just in time. Cats were starting to hunt in the deep pools of dark in the valley. On the top of the hill at Abu Ghosh, where Abinadab's house might have been, there is a rather ugly Roman Catholic church, built in the 1920s and beautifully cared for by the Sisters of St Joseph of the Apparition. It is called the church of 'Our Lady, Ark of the Covenant'. A massive statue, visible from miles away, explains the name. It shows the Ark, right enough, but standing on top of the Ark is the Virgin Mary. She cradles the baby Jesus, who holds in one hand the Sinai tablets, and in the other a piece of manna. Mary, the statue screamed, is the *real* box used to carry God around. Those old stories were just pointing to Jesus. He is the real manna: the living bread. Eat him if you want to stay alive. He is the real lawmaker, and only through him can you hope to keep the law.

'How does that make you feel?' I asked Lee. From the loudspeakers of a minaret a muezzin recorded in Mecca called the Muslim faithful to evening prayers. 'A lot of people are trying to tell me I'm behind the times,' he said. 'But we've outlasted a lot of them.'

'It might sound naïve to have a box as the vehicle of our God,' a young American rabbi had said one earnest Shabbat-night dinner in Jerusalem. 'But it's better than using our box as the vehicle for your theology.' His thinly bearded disciples put down their glasses and clapped, and looked to me for a response. What he meant was that the Ark has been hijacked by non-Jewish religions as a way of asserting that Judaism is hopelessly out of date. The beaming Madonna of Kiriath-Jearim is a good example, but there are plenty of others. Before Nablus became deadly you could see wild-eyed Ark-hunting men squinting through sextants and triangulating intensely away on Mount Gerizim. They were there because of the Samaritan tradition, recorded by Josephus, that it was on Gerizim that Moses buried the vessels – arguably including the Ark. Another Samaritan legend – in the *Memar Marqah* – has the Ark being hidden by the high priest, Uzzi, after the death of Moses. The Ark hunters shouldn't have wasted their time. The Samaritan story is theology, not history. It's supposed to be a map of buried spiritual, not actual, treasure. The point is clear: after the death of Moses God frowns on the land. The land has a hope of redemption, and the keepers of the keys of redemption are the faithful Samaritans.

Islam is even more explicit. It talks about the Mahdi, who will appear in the end times. The Koran quotes the Prophet as saying of the Mahdi: 'The sign of his kingship is that the Ark will come to you, containing serenity from your Lord and certain relics left by the families of Musa [Moses] and Harun [Aharon]. It will be borne by angels. There is a sign for you in that if you believe.' So the finding of the Ark is a mark of the truly ordained messenger of Allah. There is a fairly strong tradition, embodied in the *Hadiths*, that the Ark is in Lake Tiberias – the Sea of Galilee. Shaikh Jamaluddin was quite clear: 'The Mahdi will remove the Ark of the Covenant from Lake Tiberias.' But others seem to be equally clear that it is elsewhere: 'The reason he will be known as the Mahdi is that he will show the way to a hidden thing. He will bring the Ark to light from a place called Antioch', says one Hadith. Other Islamic scholars have placed the Ark in Jerusalem, Mecca and Istanbul. 'These separate place names may mean that the site is not known for sure and is perhaps under special protection for the Mahdi', one Islamic website cautiously suggests, adding 'Almighty Allah knows best.'

While the Ark was sitting quietly at Kiriath-Jearim in the equivalent of a suburban garage, not smiting, not plaguing, and being reverently served by Eleazar, Israel (against the advice of God, relayed through Samuel) demanded a king. They got one: his name was Saul, but he hardly comes into this story. Saul seems to have seen the Ark as a tool – a weapon of mass destruction. It went out with the Israelite army on campaign. He doesn't seem to have thought of the Ark as a focus of obligation – as a thing to be served rather than to serve. But then he increasingly had thoughts of no one except Saul.

But David was different. Steadfastly loyal to King Saul, who repeatedly tried to kill him, after Saul's death he was anointed King over all Israel at Hebron. He established Jerusalem as his capital and one of his very first acts as King, after a sortie against the Philistines, was to bring the Ark to Jerusalem.

CHAPTER 7
Up to the Mountain

Come, let us go up to the mountain of the Lord, to the
House of the God of Jacob.

Micah 4:2

...when the Temple had been erected in the likeness of
the Temple that is above, The Holy One, blessed be He,
then experienced such joy as He had not known since the
creation of the world...

Zohar, Terumah

...when the Holy One created the world, He divided it
into two parts: one part that should be habitable and the
other a desert, the former part on one side and the latter
at the other. Then He redivided the habitable part in such
a manner as it formed a circle, the centre of which is the
Holy Land. The centre of the Holy Land is Jerusalem,
and, again, the centre of Jerusalem is the Holy of
Holies... The domain of the mystery of the Faith is in that
very central point of the Holy Land which is in the Holy
of Holies, the place where the Shekinah dwelt, and even
though She dwells there no longer, and the Holy of Holies
exists no more, yet for Her sake the whole world is still
supplied with food, and nourishment and satisfaction ever
stream forth, emanating from thence to all the inhabited
regions of the world...

Zohar, Terumah

It was an immense procession. A great multitude of Israel's great and good went to that little provincial house in Kiriath-Jearim where the Ark sat. They loaded it onto the back of a new cart, and Uzzah and Ahio, the two sons of Abinadab, drove the cart. This was no staid Anglican non-festival. It was a wild charismatic praise-fest: 'David and all the house of Israel were dancing before the Lord with all their might, with songs and lyres and harps and tambourines and castanets and cymbals.' It looked as if it was all coming right.

But in the middle of the party a most horrible thing happened. The Ark was rocking about on the cart, and Uzzah, trying to be helpful, reached out and took hold of the Ark to steady it. He apparently deserved not gratitude, but instant death: 'The anger of the Lord was kindled against Uzzah; and God struck him there because he reached out his hand to the Ark; and he died there beside the Ark of God.'

This is one of the hardest things in the whole of the Ark story to stomach. 'That's not the sort of God I want to have any dealings with, Chris had said in Sinai when I told him the story. 'God's not obviously behaving there as the compassionate protector of Israel,' said Lee. 'You'd have thought he might have stretched a point on the ceremonial niceties and looked to the heart of the guy, not his hands.' And David's reaction, says the Bible, with remarkable candour, was exactly the same: 'David was angry because the Lord had burst forth with an outburst upon Uzzah...' That anger was anger against God. The invariable theological justification for Uzzah's death is to say that it underlines the terrible holiness of God. The Ark should never have been on a cart at all, says the Midrash: it should have been carried on the shoulders of

Levites. All no doubt true, but all sorts of emotional and the-ological questions are left hanging. David's anger legitimizes ours.

David was also fearful. His response was to postpone the plan to bring the Ark to Jerusalem and to put it into quarantine. It's not clear what he hoped to achieve by this. Perhaps he hoped to find out more about the dangerous properties of the Ark, and how to deal with them. Perhaps he wanted to check that the rituals he had in mind for the service of the Ark were suitable, and that its priests were properly trained. Perhaps he wanted to check that the Ark's place in Jerusalem was properly consecrated. But whatever the reason, he left the Ark for three months in the house of Obed-Edom the Gittite. We don't know who this man was, and we don't know where his house was. We're told, though, that 'the Lord blessed Obed-Edom and his household.'

Perhaps reassured by this blessing, David decided to bring the Ark up to Jerusalem. And this time he did. We're told, rather cryptically, that 'when those who bore the Ark of the Lord had gone six paces, he sacrificed an ox and a fatling.' This may mean that for every six paces of distance there was a sacrifice. A lot of blood had been shed getting the Ark to Jerusalem, and this was the last of it. There was shouting and the sound of trumpets, and David, girded with a linen ephod, 'danced before the Lord with all his might'. Saul's po-faced daughter Michal, in a metaphorical black Sunday suit, disapproved of all this unseemly religious enthusiasm. She was struck barren for her disapproval.

The Ark was placed in a tent, presumably near the Royal Palace in the City of David, which extends southwards from the present Temple Mount.

In the old City of David the weight of the aeons is suffocating. It is a tongue of land sticking out into the desert, paced by soldiers, dogs and dreamers. It is often empty these days. On one level there is not a lot to see. But then there never really was. And that's the point of going. In its heyday it must have looked like the Arab village of Silwan, just across the Kidron Valley, and nobody would bother going to Silwan, even if they weren't showered with half-bricks and their cars weren't torched. It was this dowdy little patch that God loved so passionately. A lot of the Psalms are poems about this dusty, provincial ridge. It is and always was a million aesthetic miles from Mecca and St Peter's. Jahweh has a very strange taste in cities and men.

But when all is said, God is God, and David knew it. A tent-dwelling God was all very well for a Bedouin people, but the land was won, and David slept more often on a gilded couch than a military groundsheet. 'I am living in a house of cedar,' he said to Nathan, full of self-reproach, 'but the Ark of God stays in a tent.' His intentions were firm and good. He bought from a man called Araunah a threshing-floor situated just to the north of the City of David, and had it in mind to build the Temple there. But it was not to be. That was left to David's son, Solomon.

Araunah's threshing-floor is, square foot for square foot, probably the most important plot of land in the world. If the planet goes up in a nuclear conflagration, it might very well be because of that plot.

The best place to see it is from the Mount of Olives, and the best time to go there is early in the morning or in the cool of the evening. The best way to get there is to go on foot out of the Lion Gate, take the road across the Kidron valley, and then walk up on the serpentine road past the Garden of Gethsemane, where Jesus chose to drink the cup of suffering, past the onion-domed Russian church, cut steeply up past the Church of Dominus Flevit, where Jesus is said to have wept over Jerusalem, and up onto the ridge. This is a hill of graves. Often you will see a black-coated Hasidic funeral party in the huge Jewish cemetery, or individual mourners come to put a stone on the grave, for the stones cry out to God in this city. The Messiah, like the rising sun, will come into the Holy City from the east, up through the sealed Golden Gate, as Jesus did on the donkey. The dead will rise at his feet, so those buried on the Mount of Olives are the first fruits of Messianic redemption. The Kidron valley itself, in some traditions, is the valley of judgment. In some stories the dead walk on a tightrope slung across the valley, and if you are overbalanced by your sins you topple down and gnash your teeth in the desert instead of feasting in the city. The dominance of the citizen over the nomad is the rule in death as in life.

But when you look down from the ridge you do not see the Kidron or the graves or the garden of suffering and obedience, or the grey dome of the Church of the Holy Sepulchre. You can, but you don't. You don't see, either, the seething, creaking, dancing, screaming city that surges round these places. You join in the universal tunnel vision that sees only a dazzling golden dome. This is the dome that stands iconically on the TV screens whenever the Israeli–Palestinian conflict is being discussed. It is the dome that stands wistfully and provocatively on Muslim calendars: wistfully because the Dome is in tragically occupied Palestine; provocatively because the third holiest shrine of Islam stands subversively right at the heart of the enemy camp, on the very place where the enemy's Temple stood. And without its Temple, the enemy has no mechanism of salvation. It is the Dome of the Rock, one of the very earliest statements of Islam about itself: built in the shape of a Byzantine church to show that Islam was the true church, and made far more magnificent than any church or synagogue to make it clear to everyone that Allah had won.

If you go to certain shops in the Jewish Quarter you can buy other views. One of the most popular is a conventional photograph of the Temple Mount and the Old City with the tower blocks and hotels of west Jerusalem rising behind. But on this photograph there is no Dome of the Rock. Nor is there an Al-Aqsa mosque beside it. Instead, where the Dome of the Rock stands, there is a huge, rectangular colonnaded building. Outside it, white-robed priests process and debate, and the smoke of sacrifice drifts gently to heaven. This is the vision of an increasingly vocal, influential and well-organized minority within ultra-orthodox Judaism. They periodically process up to the Temple Mount carrying the cornerstone of the next Temple, and are firmly and none too politely turned back by the Israeli Army. But it is more than just a stunt. They are in deadly earnest.

If you are coming from the east, the eastern wall of the Temple Mount is the first really urban thing that you hit for a thousand miles or more. There's a sprinkling of development along the Olivet ridge and the slopes just beyond it, but it doesn't amount to much. Until then it has been relentless wilderness. And suddenly not only does the wilderness end, but you are in the antithesis of wilderness: you are in the quintessential Garden, a reconstructed Eden.

At least that is how God and Solomon saw it. Everywhere in the Temple were engravings of cherubim, palm trees and open flowers. The cherubim guarded the entrance to Eden, overshadowed the Ark, and now looked down from every wall. Man had been banished from the original Eden, and the cherubim kept him from returning. Now an acceptable propitiatory sacrifice could be offered, man could return, and the cherubim were there in the new Eden to greet him rather than forbid him.

Something else happened in the dark, said the rabbis. Surrounded by flowers, Jahweh lay with his beloved on the couch that was the Ark. The Holy of Holies was the love-chamber of the Song of Songs. Metaphors got mixed over the centuries: sometimes the Ark was the bed; sometimes the Lady Ark was the spirit of the Beloved Jerusalem.

This was the perfect place of sacrifice. The rock at the heart of the Temple was, said Jewish tradition, Mount Moriah, where Abraham had offered Isaac. It was the navel of the whole world, and so a sacrifice offered here might be effective not just for men but for the whole creation of which man was the apex. The Temple was both Eden restored and the means of restoring Eden; it was not just Adam restored and the means of his redemption. Beneath the Rock, now shackled and subdued by the Creator, roared the primeval waters of chaos that had covered the earth at the time of creation and had been unleashed to drown the disobedient at the time of Noah.

The Temple, says the Bible, took seven years to build. That may have been a symbolic seven years, denoting the divine correspondence between its construction and God's construction of the world. Perhaps the symbolic was actual.

The building involved slave labour on a Pharaonic scale and massive foreign imports, particularly of cedar from Lebanon. But eventually it was done, and the Temple was dedicated. The Ark was at the heart of the dedication. The Bible's account reads very much like a dedication of a house for the Ark:

> Then Solomon assembled the elders of Israel and all the heads of the tribes, the leaders of the ancestral houses of the Israelites, before King Solomon in Jerusalem, to bring up the Ark of the Covenant of the Lord out of the city of David, which is Zion. All the people of Israel assembled to King Solomon at the festival in the month Ethanim, which is the seventh month. And all the elders of Israel came, and the priests came, and the priests carried the Ark. So they brought up the Ark of the Lord, the tent of meeting and all the holy vessels that were in the tent; the priests and the Levites brought them up. King Solomon and all the congregation of Israel, who had assembled before him, were with him before the Ark, sacrificing so many sheep and oxen that they could not be counted or numbered. Then the priests brought the Ark of the Covenant of the Lord to its place in the inner sanctuary of the house, in the most holy place, underneath the wings of the cherubim. For the cherubim spread out their wings over the place of the Ark, so that the cherubim made a covering above the Ark and its poles. The poles were so long that the ends of the poles were seen from the holy place in front of the inner sanctuary; but they could not be seen from outside; they are there to this day. There was nothing in the Ark except the two tablets of stone that Moses had placed there at Horeb, where the Lord made a covenant with the Israelites, when they came out of the land of Egypt. And when the priests came out of the holy place, a cloud filled the house of the Lord, so

> that the priests could not stand to minister because of the
> cloud; for the glory of the Lord filled the house of the
> Lord. Then Solomon said: 'The Lord has said that he
> would dwell in thick darkness. I have built for you an
> exalted house, a place for you to dwell in forever.'

This is moving and beautiful, but also theologically disquieting. Should God need a house? Solomon felt the disquiet too,
and raised the point in his prayer of dedication: 'But will God
indeed dwell on the earth? Even heaven and the highest
heaven cannot contain you, much less this house that I have
built... Hear the plea of your servant and of your people
Israel when they pray toward this place; O hear in heaven
your dwelling place...' But to be aware of an objection is not
to answer it, and Solomon has not answered it here. If God
lives in heaven, what is in the Holy of Holies? If God is everywhere, is he more intensely present in the Temple than anywhere else? What is the Ark all about? There is a clear
tension between the view of God expressed in Solomon's
prayer and the view of God expressed in the whole idea of
the Temple and cultic worship. The tension has never been
satisfactorily resolved. It was to cause spectacular ructions in
the time of King Josiah. But for the moment the cultic,
priestly view of the Temple and the Ark prevailed.

And so, for centuries, the Ark that had been carried by
the Israelites from Sinai seems to have stood in the deep dark
of the Holy of Holies; a dark so incomprehensibly deep that
later rabbis spoke of it as the primordial light from which all
other light sprang. The Ark itself was approached only once
a year, on Yom Kippur, the Day of Atonement, when the
High Priest walked before it in a cloud of incense to sprinkle
the atoning sacrificial bull blood. The High Priest groped his

way to the Ark along the poles and, according to some stories, had a rope round his ankle so that if he was struck dead
he could be pulled out of the sanctuary.

Many ultra-orthodox Jews today wouldn't go onto the
Temple Mount, even if they could. We don't know the exact
place of the Holy of Holies, they say, and we might inadver-
tently commit the lethal blasphemy of walking over it. If the
Dutch archaeological draughtsman Leen Ritmeyer is right,
though, they need not worry. He is the world's authority on
the structure of the Temple. I managed to track him down on
the phone.

'There's a long tradition that the rock in the centre of the
Dome of the Rock, known by the Arabs simply as "es-Sakhra"
– "the Rock" – was the bedrock platform which was inside
the Holy of Holies,' he said. 'There are no other obvious candidates, and it seems to fit. I was on a flight to Israel once,
and, bored, I took out a photograph of the Sakhra. I looked
closely at the area where I thought the Holy of Holies was,
and inside, right in the centre, was something I hadn't ever
noticed before. It was a rectangular shadow. I got out a ruler
and measured it. Its measurements accorded exactly with the
dimensions of the Ark of the Covenant as the Bible gives
them. It was clear now what it was: this was a flattened area
on which the Ark had stood – fashioned specially to stop it
rocking about. It was the most exciting flight I had ever had.'

So that was where the Ark stood, at the epicentre of a gigan-
tic liturgical abattoir, dowsed in blood, worshipped in the
screams of bulls and goats and in the prayers of the desperate: brooding, angry, merciful, terrible and benevolent.

And then it went missing. Almost everyone agrees that

there was no Ark in the Temple that was built to replace Solomon's Temple, which was destroyed by the Babylonians. Most think that it went missing at or around that time, and there are some very interesting speculations about where it might have ended up. But there are some who think that for almost all the time that bulls were killed for the Ark in Solomon's Temple, there was no Ark there at all.

CHAPTER 8

The Jewel in Sheba's Crown

...King Solomon gave to the queen of Sheba every desire
that she expressed, as well as what he gave her out of
Solomon's royal bounty. Then she returned to her own
land, with her servants.

1 Kings 10:13

As the plane makes its approach to Addis Ababa,
you see that Ethiopia moves all the time, jigging
up and down with mules and swaying side to side
with camels. As soon as the plane doors open, the smell of
Africa comes at you: the smell of decay and unimaginable
fecundity; despair and absurd aspiration. The women wear
dazzling necklaces of sweat, and the children have an intimidating self-possession. It is intimidating because, although
they have nothing to eat, they clearly know something very
important that I don't know. When they talk, it is like Arabic
played on a glass xylophone. There are ragged hills in a broken frill around Addis Ababa, but there is more horizon than
land, and so a queasy sense of being poised on the edge of
some huge void.

In the morning I waited in a packed eating-house, where I was the only one eating because everyone else was busy watching me. And in the afternoon I waited in a bar. It was one of those anonymous no man's lands between worlds in which I seem to have spent a lot of life. Furniture from nowhere; drinks from duty free; loud men in stained safari suits from everywhere but here; the antiseptic voice of some self-satisfied CNN anchorwoman being relayed from a transmitter in Djibouti. It was an alcoholic Wood-Between-the-Worlds, with everyone on an expense account. While a couple of thousand children died of hunger outside, I drank some tremendous Ethiopian red wine made in the famine region of Awash.

I was happy to wait. Whenever I fly out of Heathrow it takes a bit of time for my brain to come out of spasm and begin to be able to intuit again. I do terrible, abusive things to it in England – making it jump through hoops it was never designed to go through: dangerously over-exercising it in some areas; dangerously under-exercising it in others. And it reacts just like any other tired tissue.

Eventually Keith arrived. Eventually Keith always does. I'd last seen him in the Sahara, where we'd rubbed surgical spirit into the wounds on each other's feet, run along a line of flares through many a long night and sworn that we'd never go south of Kent ever again.

We ate some condemned meat in a café owned by a boss-eyed former beauty who had earned her fortune as the concubine of a minor Arabian prince, and we stared into the dark. The candles and the paraffin lamps make every face tragic: they turn the little lines on the children's faces into furrows. Every Ethiopian woman over thirty is a Gagool after dusk. A heavy cloud of incense seeps from half the houses. It coils around the necks of the people inside, and blurs their bodies so you see their heads on a platter of smoke. The incense glows the same colour as hyenas' eyes. They burn the same incense as they burn in the little Ethiopian chapel on the roof of the Holy Sepulchre Church in Jerusalem. It was in the darkness of that chapel, heavy with age and holiness and poverty, that I first knew the panic and the comfort that comes from the taste of great antiquity.

Even in the white heat of the day there is still darkness in the huts and under the tents. Darkness is the one thing the country protects successfully. When the night comes, the land is one vast hut. Switch on the Land Rover lights and you see couples sitting everywhere in the dust, whispering and laughing and sitting silently, watching the dark together.

Some say that the Ark went into this great darkness, and stayed here. Those Ethiopian priests in Jerusalem, long before I was interested in the Ark, had pointed to a bad coloured lithograph of the Ark, beamed and said: 'We have it at home.' That opinion is universal amongst Ethiopians and widespread amongst the readers of station-bookstall bestsellers.

There are many more or less exotic variations on the basic theme. The traditional story, believed by the Ethiopian Orthodox with all the fire and a lot more of the certainty with which they believe the doctrine of the Trinity, is based on *The Glory of the Kings* (the *Kebra Nagast*), the Ethiopian national epic. Its starting point is the visit of the Queen of Sheba to King Solomon. The Bible itself tells of the visit, using the Queen (who may well have come from the Yemen) as a literary voicebox to extol the splendour, riches and wisdom of Solomon. But the *Kebra Nagast* goes a lot further. The

Queen, there, is the virgin queen of Ethiopia, called Makeda. Having heard of Solomon's magnificence and munificence, she makes the journey to Jerusalem. She is entranced by Solomon, and he is pretty impressed by her too. He explains to her that he has all this wisdom, wealth and power because he is a slave – a slave to his Lady, the Ark of the Covenant. Makeda stays for six months: her relationship with Solomon is that of disciple and guru. When she is about to leave, Solomon tricks her out of her virginity, which she is hardly reluctant to lose. Laden with gifts, including a ring to be worn by any child conceived during their night of passion, she returns to rule her people.

Makeda duly bears a son, and calls him Bayna-Lehkem, or Menelik. As a child he discovers who his father is, and when he is twenty-one he goes to Jerusalem to meet Solomon, bearing the ring that proves Solomon's paternity.

Solomon is astonished at Menelik's resemblance to his own father, David. He grows very fond of the boy, urging him to stay in Jerusalem. But Menelik is firm: he has only come to Jerusalem to learn wisdom at his father's feet, and must return to Ethiopia. Solomon reluctantly agrees: the eldest sons of Israel's leading men are to go with Menelik to Ethiopia, where they will help him to rule in a Solomonic way. Zadok the Priest, who anointed Solomon King of Israel, now inducts Menelik into the line of the Davidic kings, even changing his name to David.

While preparations are afoot for David's journey, a conspiracy is brewing amongst the young men who are to go with him. They decide that they simply cannot be parted from the Ark. Azarias, the son of Zadok, suggests that they take the Ark with them. A crude wooden replica is made, and placed beneath the ritual cloth that covers the Ark. The true Ark is buried in a hole in the ground until the party is ready to leave. The plan is endorsed and encouraged by the Angel of the Lord. They will have no trouble, he says, because the Ark has itself decided to go to Ethiopia. God, in other words, has a new Chosen People.

The Ark is put on a cart, concealed beneath a pile of dirty washing, and then the party moves off. The trick has not yet been discovered, but already the city and its king are in the grip of a strange despair. Solomon realizes that something has changed: something has left him. The political message of the story could not be clearer: the divine endorsement of Solomon's dynasty has been transferred to a more faithful people – the Ethiopians. The Lady Zion has been enthroned in a New African Jerusalem.

The Archangel Gabriel is at the head of the curious caravan as it makes its way south-westwards. They fly through the air, the angels of Mount Sinai serenade them as they go past, and the waters of the Red Sea roar for joy, celebrating the journey of the Ark to its proper home. David, who has not been party to the conspiracy, is told by his companions what has happened. He is ecstatic, and dances before the Ark as his grandfather had done. The gargantuan idols of Egypt shudder and crumble as the Ark passes over them.

Back in Jerusalem, the plot is discovered, and Solomon, devastated, orders his horsemen to ride after the Ark, bring David back to Jerusalem and kill the other thieves. But he is far too late. The fleetest horses of the Israelite cavalry are no match for supernatural flight.

What is to be done? Will the Israelites continue to support the Davidic monarchy if they know that there is no Ark?

The safest course, Solomon and the elders decide, is to pretend that nothing has happened. The crude Ark left by the conspirators is covered in gold, decorated like the original Ark, and left in the sanctuary. But Solomon knows the truth. The Ark was the source of his wisdom. Without it, he declines. That is where the Bible picks up the story again. Solomon does indeed lose his wisdom: he runs after foreign women, gets ensnared by their gods, and loses the favour of Jahweh.

Ethiopia is transformed by the arrival of the Ark. Idols are smashed; immorality is banished; the God of Israel is truly worshipped in this true Israel. Ethiopia's enemies wither before David and the Ark. And, the true believers say, the Ark is now in the disappointingly uncharismatic Chapel of the Tablet in Aksum, built in 1965 by Emperor Haile Selassie and designed by architects who ought to be shot and very possibly were. It is watched over by a monastic guardian, appointed for life by the previous guardian. The Ark is taken out of the Chapel once a year for the ceremony of *Timkat*, and processed around the town in an orgiastic festival which makes the dancing of the original King David look funereal. The Ark, say the Ethiopians, does for Ethiopia what it has always done. It has kept her as a special nation: a Christian island in a raging sea of paganism.

There are five massive problems in regarding the *Kebra Nagast* as history. The first is the obviously mythological tone of the narrative: the Ark flies; it defeats a city populated by human-headed asps with donkeys' tails hanging out of their bellies. The second is that it is very ham-fistedly political. It has an obvious agenda, to which every detail of the narrative is subservient. It is designed to establish the divinely endorsed legitimacy of the Ethiopian monarchy. It says plainly that to oppose the monarchy is to oppose God himself. The third is the date: it is a medieval document which seems to have appeared sometime in the thirteenth century AD – a time when the Aksumite monarchy of Ethiopia was under serious threat. The fourth is that we have some careful early descriptions of the Ethiopian Ark, and it is obviously a Christian object. In the thirteenth century AD the Armenian traveller Abu Salih saw the Ark in use. He wrote:

> The Abyssinians possess also the Ark of the Covenant, in which are the two tablets of stone, inscribed by the finger of God with the commandments which he ordained for the children of Israel. The Ark of the Covenant is placed upon the altar, but it is not so wide as the altar; it is as high as the knee of a man, and is overlaid by gold; and upon its upper cover there are crosses of gold; and there are five precious stones upon it, one at each of the four corners, and one in the middle.

He was writing long before Ark tourism made the Ethiopians secretive about the Ark: there is no reason to suppose that he was describing anything other than the 'real' Ethiopian Ark.

And the fifth problem we shall come to in more detail: it is that there is evidence that the Ark was present in the Temple until – well, until well after the reign of Solomon, and that the cover-up suggested by the *Kebra Nagast* is unlikely to have occurred.

These and other difficulties with the *Kebra Nagast* have led other writers, notably Graham Hancock, to suggest alternative explanations for the presence of the Ark in Ethiopia. But why assume that it is there at all? It seems to me that no one would ever have begun to think that it was there, and accordingly that its presence required an explanation, if it had not been for the *Kebra Nagast*'s insistence that it was. Damage the credibility of the *Kebra Nagast*, and you inevitably damage the credibility of all the other Ethiopian Ark theorists, including those like Hancock who reject the *Kebra Nagast*'s account.

The drive south from Mekele was interesting. Clouds crashed, and we never saw the road for cocoa waves of storm-water. We parked up for a cup of tea, and just managed to get back to the Land Rover before the village drain, grown to a cataract, took it off to Egypt. A few hours further down we had to cross a bridge, but its back was broken. They were trying to fix it. We waited for an hour and then got bored and found that Land Rovers can float. After that it was a bit like South Vietnam: flat fields of *tef* and wrecked tanks; overloaded bicycles and draught cows and leprosy and pale, tall birds eating dead dogs. Then up again on a stomach-churning ribbon of a road sliding in the rain into the air. We hit the plateau, missed our turn and spent a night shivering on the concrete floor of a goat-pen.

Early the next morning we drove through the red hills of Lasta to the city of Lalibela, a sort of medieval Christian theme park. The Ethiopian Prince, Lalibela, went to Jerusalem in 1160 as a political exile. He stayed there for twenty-five years, and was impressed, as well he might be. So when he came back to Ethiopia he decided to recreate the whole thing. So you can go to Golgotha, Bethlehem, Mount Tabor, the River Jordan and all the main New Testament sites. The children, at least, take the whole thing very literally. 'That,' they tell you, in exchange for a biro, 'is where Jesus spent his last night on earth.' It is all underground, hewn straight out of the rock by, depending on whom you believe, 40,000 Ethiopians, a legion of (pretty cack-handed) angels (overnight) or some mysterious, red-haired, white-faced knights who had followed the trail of the Ark of the Covenant all the way from Jerusalem. They were from the Order of the Poor Knights of Christ and of the Temple of Solomon. They are better known as the Knights Templar.

It is true that the churches at Lalibela are supreme, pre-cocious architectural achievements, and that almost nothing is known for sure about how or when they were made. It is true that there have been persistent rumours of the involve-ment of white men in their construction, and that the name of the Templars has often been anecdotally linked to them. But once that is said, all is said. There is plenty of specula-tion, though, and the most sustained and articulate specula-tion is Graham Hancock's. His book *The Sign and the Seal* put the Ethiopian Ark thesis on the mental map of millions and hugely inflated the profits of hoteliers and postcard manufac-turers in northern Ethiopia. He is a persuasive advocate, and his argument is so tightly woven that it is sometimes hard to see the massive, groundless assumptions.

Jerusalem was captured by the Crusaders in 1099. In 1199 nine French noblemen went to Jerusalem and were welcomed by the Crusader King, Baldwin I, who let them establish their headquarters on the Temple Mount. This was certainly a great privilege: many have construed from it a specific mission – to search for hidden secrets on and under the Temple Mount. For about seven years the Knights did something in and around the Temple Mount. They rarely left it, and it certainly seems unlikely that they could have done much to guard the road linking Jerusalem to the coase – their official reason for being in the Holy Land. Shortly after this period of sequestered obscurity the Templars acquired huge wealth and influence, running a sophisticated system of international banking, owning great estates and having the ear of the Pope himself.

So what were they doing? There is evidence that they were involved in some excavation. A tunnel burrowing into the Temple Mount from the south has been found to contain Templar artefacts, and many, including Leen Ritmeyer, think that tunnelling under the Sakhra in the Dome of the Rock was the work of the Templars. So what did they find? Not the Ark, according to Hancock: if they had found that, he says, they would not have failed to trumpet news of the discovery across Christendom. Others think that they came across some of the hidden treasure from Solomon's Temple – hidden in circumstances to which we will come. But Hancock thinks that they found some esoteric architectural secrets – the secrets used in the construction of Solomon's Temple itself.

It is true that the Templars proved to be superb architects and builders, and of course modern Freemasons trace their origins back to the Templars and their arcane Solomonic knowledge. Depending on how fanciful you are, you can then choose to believe, supported by many a lucrative paperback, that these secrets had been exported from Egypt, where they had been used to build the astonishing monuments of the Pharaohs, and that in turn the secrets derived from the lost civilization of Atlantis. But Hancock is not so fanciful. He notes, plausibly enough, that the rise of the Templars coincided with the rise of Gothic architecture in Europe – a movement, he says, which seemed to come out of nowhere, and at the heart of which was the notion that certain relations of height, breadth and depth reflected the perfect harmony of God. He also noted that the rise of the Templars depended crucially on the patronage of Bernard of Clairvaux, one of the prime movers of the Gothic movement. Put it all together, he says, and you can conclude that the Templars traded their Solomonic knowledge for Bernard's help.

That is all very well, but he is still a long way from Ethiopia. He never really gets his argument comfortably across the Red Sea. He sees some faded, red-paint crosses in the Church of Beta Mariam which look to him like Templar crosses. He thinks that Lalibela is so architecturally impressive that it must have been built with outside help (although no one has seriously suggested that there is anything quintessentially Euro-Gothic about it). He notes that Father Francisco Alvarez, who accompanied a Portuguese mission to Ethiopia in 1520–26, mentioned a tradition that Lalibela had been built by white men, and further relies on a letter of 1165, supposedly written by 'Prester John' and almost universally regarded as a hoax, which urges the King of France to 'put to death those treacherous Templars.' This letter, says Hancock, was genuinely from Ethiopia, from Harbay, Lalibela's half brother, and it indicated that Templars were in Ethiopia causing trouble.

But even if all this is true, where does it leave us? Suppose there were Templars in Ethiopia sometime in the twelfth century, searching frantically for the Ark that they had failed to find in Jerusalem. What evidence is there that they found it there? None at all, unless you presume (and it would be a rank presumption) that the treachery referred to in the probably forged letter of Prester John was attempted theft of the

Ark – or something that they, rightly or wrongly, thought was the Ark. Hancock does his best to say that the Grail legends that proliferated at the time of the Crusades are really Ark legends, to which the obvious response is: possibly, but so what? He contends too that there are some clues in the cathedral at Chartres which suggest that the builders knew of the *Kebra Nagast* legend. But again, so what? Knowledge of a legend is hardly evidence of its truth. And he's expressly said that the *Kebra Nagast*, except insofar as it asserts that the Ark is in Ethiopia, is untrue.

Where he does get interesting, however, is in his account of the religious practices of the Falashas – the black Jews of Ethiopia, most of whom are now in Israel. There are three really significant things: the Falashas don't celebrate Hanukkah; they don't celebrate Purim; and, at least until the nineteenth century AD, they performed animal sacrifice. To see why this matters we need to go back to Jerusalem, but dropping off in Egypt.

The best way to get to Aswan is on the sleeper from Cairo, and that is the way I always go. The train hugs the Nile, as Egyptian history has done. You never really sleep, but you are never really awake. The starched tablecloths in the dining car are limp by the time you get to Beni Suef; they sometimes sell liver and onions; the waiters have loosened their bow-ties by Minya and taken them off by Asyut; and as you approach Aswan station there is always a family of bee-eaters on the wires.

The best view, the best lemon-juice and the worst company in Aswan are in the Old Cataract Hotel. Now I slumped on the terrace, fooling nobody that I could afford to stay there, listening to a lino salesman from Luton bickering with his mistress about how much of the love-nest mortgage she should pay, and watching the feluccas drift across the Nile to Elephantine Island. I had spent an arduous afternoon there, trying to make sense of the excavations. Not many people are bothered with them: they are the least visually spectacular ruins for a thousand miles in any direction. But they matter very much indeed. This is because there is a temple there. And it is Jewish.

It was built in the second half of the seventh or at the beginning of the sixth century BC, and destroyed in 410 BC. It was big, rich, a centre for propitiatory animal sacrifices, and papyri speak of Yahu (Jahweh) as dwelling there. And all that, according to the decrees of King Josiah of Judah, was blasphemous anathema.

After the death of Solomon things were never the same again. The Kingdom was big, splendid and overstretched. It went downhill, splitting into the northern Kingdom of Israel, with its capital at Samaria, and the southern Kingdom of Judah, with its capital at Jerusalem. The two Kingdoms were frequently at odds, but it is mostly Judah that concerns us. The northern Kingdom fell to the Assyrians in 722/721 BC, and its inhabitants were carried off into captivity, never to return again (unless you think that the modern State of Israel really is the ingathering of the Ten Lost Tribes plus the others).

The Bible is often subtle, but in its portraits of Judah's kings it most certainly is not. The kings were almost alternately Good and Bad until you get to Josiah. He was very, very Good, and everyone after him was very, very Bad. The Good ones were the ones who were faithful to Jahweh. The Bad ones flirted with and often slept with foreign gods, neglected the worship in the Temple, and worse. We come across a couple of them later.

Far and away the best of the Good was King Josiah (640–609 BC). He was a reforming religious zealot. His reforms were fuelled by the finding of the 'Book of the Law' in the Temple – found because he had the piety to repair the Temple. This Book purported to be the law as given to Moses, and is generally thought to be the Book of Deuteronomy; certainly the spirit of Deuteronomy conforms perfectly to the Bible's picture of Josiah. The Book of the Law has returned to ensure that the law returns. And Josiah takes the commission very seriously indeed. He's a sort of Near Eastern Cromwell. He holds public Bible-readings, and pledges that he and his people will hold fast to the law. He deposes idolatrous priests; he pounds idols to dust; he defiles the high places where false gods had been worshipped; he restores the festival of Passover, which had fallen into abeyance.

The God of Deuteronomy is stony-faced and Presbyterian. He is intensely concerned about morality, jealously anxious to ensure that only he is worshipped, and suspicious of the cult of Temple worship. Until Josiah the theology of Jerusalem had been the theology of the books of Numbers and Exodus: descriptive, unsystematic and tribal. No systematic theology can begin to describe the raging, surprising and apparently capricious God of Numbers. Systematic theology was born in Deuteronomy. You might not like the picture of Jahweh that emerges there; you might like even less the totalitarian zeal of the humourless Josiah, and long for the flawed but red-blooded David; but at least it is possible to begin to make general statements about the Deuteronomist's Jahweh – to philosophize about him.

The different voices of Deuteronomy and Numbers/Exodus are heard best when they talk about the Ark. For the Deuteronomist the Ark is a filing cabinet. Its significance lies in what it holds: the tablets of the law. The Deuteronomist would sympathize strongly with the scriptural conservatives who talk with reverent dread about the Word of the Lord – meaning the written words of the Bible. The Deuteronomist's Ark is a plain wooden box. The Ark of Exodus and Numbers is very different: it is covered in gorgeous gold, and crowned with cherubim. It appears to be an object of veneration in its own right; the apotheosis of that veneration was of course Solomon's Temple in Jerusalem. Because of this obvious discrepancy it has been suggested that there were two or more Arks, but that just won't wash.

Although he was less cultic than those of his royal predecessors who had remained faithful to Jahweh, Josiah was more fastidious. Temple worship would be reformed; there might be less mystery in it; it might seem less tangibly sacred, but it still had to be done properly. Like many reformers, Josiah was also a great controller and so a great centralizer. What happened on the Temple Mount in Jerusalem might be rather less important than a daily, faithful relationship with Jahweh, but if Temple worship were allowed to happen anywhere other than in Jerusalem, under Josiah's own eyes, who knows what abominations might recur? Theoretically, no propitiatory sacrifice could be made other than in the appointed sacrificial centre of the people – whether at the Tabernacle during the wanderings, at the Tabernacle at Shilo, or at the Temple in Jerusalem. But under

Josiah's new fundamentalism the theory became practice. He is said to have decreed that there would be sacrifice in Jerusalem and nowhere but Jerusalem. And that is why the Elephantine Temple, where I had spent the afternoon, was so significant.

Or so says Graham Hancock. It is an important pillar of his argument. The reasoning goes, of course, that if worship of and sacrifice to Jahweh were proscribed everywhere but Jerusalem, there must have been something truly exceptional to make the Elephantine Jews breach the prohibition. And what might that be? Well, the presence of the Ark, of course. The *Kebra Nagast* had it partly right: the Ark did indeed go to Ethiopia via Egypt. When the Elephantine community broke up, where did they go? There's no documentary indication, but surely up the Nile to Ethiopia, bearing the Ark: QED.

But, again, it just doesn't work. We know that the community in Elephantine was a theologically unorthodox one. It wasn't only Yahu who was worshipped there, but also two goddesses – Ashambethel and Anathbethel. Josiah would have been horrified. This was just the sort of thing that his reforms were designed to stamp out. So the community either didn't know about his reforms, or didn't care about them. If they were so heretical as to worship goddesses alongside Jahweh, we can't begin to conclude that Jahweh, in the form of the Ark, must have been the justification for Jahweh worship. But however impious those Elephantine Jews were, surely they wouldn't have been so downright stupid as to make the real Ark share quarters with some upstart goddesses.

It's not just this. Elephantine isn't the only example of an Israelite temple outside Jerusalem. There were also temples

at Araq el-Emir in Jordan and Leontopolis in Egypt. To maintain his thesis, Hancock would have to say that there was an
Ark in each of them.

What about the festivals? Hancock's point is a simple
one. Hanukkah is the celebration of the Purification of the
Temple. It celebrates the victory of Judas Maccabaeus in 164
BC. If the Falashas do not celebrate it, says Hancock, then
they cannot have had any communication with mainstream
Jewry since then. In fact we simply do not know exactly
when the celebration of Hanukkah started, except that it was
well established by the late first or early second century AD.
Purim is the celebration of the deliverance of the Jews from
the hands of the evil Haman, who sought to kill them. The
story is told in the Book of Esther. Hancock says that 'several
of the authorities whom I consulted suggested that [Purim's]
observance had become widely popular by 425 BC', and he
accordingly concludes that the Falashas were cut off from
Jerusalem by then. In fact there is no reference to the celebration of Purim in any Jewish literature before the first century BC. But even if Hancock is right about this immensely
early date for Purim celebration, the question to ask of him
will now be familiar: so what? So what if you have an isolated
island of Jews, perhaps derived from the Elephantine garrison fleeing in or around 410 BC, that lived in the highlands of
Ethiopia surrounded by an unnavigable sea of pagans and,
later, Christians? Suppose too that they persisted in some
sort of temple worship, as they did at Elephantine and as
other Jews did elsewhere. (It would be rather surprising if
they didn't.) It tells you absolutely nothing about the whereabouts of the Ark.

Hancock is canny enough not to point to Menelik's party

as the thieves of the Ark. He has another candidate. In fact, if you think that the Ark was not in Jerusalem when the Babylonians came massing around the city, you will find several possible candidates.

CHAPTER 9
Into the Ether

'There is not less treasure in the world', said Sidonia,
'because we use paper currency…'

Disraeli, *Coningsby*

Every point in Jerusalem is a beachhead, but everything is
dry and there is no ocean of water. Yet the sea of
Jerusalem is the most terrible sea of all. Every place in
Jerusalem is a tongue of the city – and the city has many
tongues and nobody understands her…

Yehuda Amichai, translated from the Hebrew by Hillel
Halkin

If Menelik didn't steal the Ark, and if the Ark was gone
by the time of the Babylonian invasion, then who did take
it? There are two commonly cited suspects: the Pharaoh
Sheshonq I (known to the Bible as King Shishak) and the
thoroughly evil King Manasseh of Judah.

Indiana Jones had no doubt. It was Shishak, he confidently told his enraptured audience. And so Steven Spielberg
went unerringly to Egypt, and Harrison Ford, without ever

taking his hat off, found it in the snake-filled vault where Shishak had left it.

This has not been a very popular thesis over the years, but it has always had adherents. Michael Sanders, for instance, recorded for the benefit of ABC television viewers his belief that Shishak had buried the stone tablets looted from the Ark in a temple dedicated to Amun Ra, now just a heap of stone in the notoriously militant West Bank village of Dhahiriya, near Hebron. The locals were not impressed and refused him permission to excavate, and Sanders returned to Irvine, California, bloody but unbowed, insisting that the greatest treasure of antiquity was there for the taking.

The Shishak hypothesis is completely unarguable. Certainly Shishak's 918/917 BC campaign against Judah, spiritually weakened in the Bible's eyes through the disastrously blasphemous rule of Solomon's son, Rehoboam, was costly for Judah. 'In the fifth year of King Rehoboam,' the First Book of Kings tells us, 'King Shishak of Egypt came up against Jerusalem; he took away the treasures of the house of the Lord and the treasures of the king's house; he took everything.' And there you have the height of the case against Shishak. It is a dismal one. It relies on the assumption that the Ark was included amongst the 'treasures of the Lord's house'. But this is unlikely. The expression seems to refer to the contents of the Temple treasury, which was not part of the Temple itself. It seems clear, too, that the really sacred treasures of the Temple – the menorah, the altar of incense and the table of shewbread – were in use shortly after the invasion: they are expressly referred to in the Second Book of Chronicles. Then there's the failure of the Bible to mention at all what would have been a colossal religious crisis. It wasn't coy about relating the capture of the Ark by the Philistines: why should it keep silent if the Ark had been seized by Shishak?

But there are two even more compelling reasons to acquit Shishak. The first is that he never entered Jerusalem at all. He was not slow to boast on his victory relief in Karnak about the cities he had taken, but Jerusalem was not amongst them. What plainly happened was that, as was common practice, Jerusalem paid tribute to Shishak in return for Shishak not besieging the city. That tribute included gold from the treasury: it is wholly inconceivable that it could have included the Ark.

And indeed we know that it did not. For the Bible subsequently mentions the Ark, still in Jerusalem, in the reign of King Josiah (640–609 BC). That mention is central to the exculpation of the next suspect, King Manasseh of Judah (c. 687/686–642 BC), whose collar is fingered by Graham Hancock.

Manasseh 'did what was evil in the sight of the Lord, following the abominable practices of the nations that the Lord drove out before the people of Israel.' He rebuilt the high places where the pagan gods were worshipped; he erected altars for Baal, and a sacred pole; he practised soothsaying and augury, consulted mediums and wizards and 'worshipped all the host of heaven and served them'. He was a fairly typical syncretistic New Ager. But what is really interesting is what he did in the Temple at Jerusalem:

> He built altars in the house of the Lord, of which the
> Lord had said, 'In Jerusalem I will put my name.' He built
> altars for all the host of heaven in the two courts of the
> house of the Lord... The carved image of Asherah that he

had made he set in the house of which the Lord said to
David and to his son Solomon, 'In this house, and in
Jerusalem, which I have chosen out of all the tribes of
Israel, I will put my name forever...'

The trees painted on the walls of the Temple withered when
the idol was brought in, says the Aggadah. The Bible citation
is taken from the Second Book of Kings, which is a prosecu-
tion document. It is keen to portray Manasseh in the worst
possible light. If Manasseh had interfered in any way with the
Ark, it would have said so. But Manasseh's sin was not to stop
worshipping Jahweh; it was the old Israelite sin of worshipping other gods as well as Jahweh. So there is no reason for
Manasseh to have banished or destroyed the Ark. It is just
possible that some members of the faithful Jahwehist
Levitical priesthood might have moved the Ark out of the
Temple during the scourge of Manasseh so that Jahweh did
not have to endure the company of false gods. But if they did,
it is clear that they moved it back in again when the theological coast was clear. And that was in or before the reign of
King Josiah.

We have met Josiah before. He was the zealous reforming king, calling Judah back to the cult-lite purity of
Deuteronomy. He ascended to the throne of Judah as an
eight-year-old boy, just two years after the death of
Manasseh, and he found plenty to get his reforming teeth
into. The Temple was purified; the abominations of
Manasseh were destroyed. And then the Second Book of
Chronicles has a very curious verse. It is the last indication in
the canonical scriptures of the earthly existence and location
of the Ark:

> [Josiah] said to the Levites who taught all Israel and who
> were holy to the Lord, 'Put the holy ark in the house that
> Solomon son of David, king of Israel, built; you need no
> longer carry it on your shoulders.'

A great deal of ink and academic bile have been spilt over this
verse. It might mean that the Levites had been keeping the
Ark safe during the difficult days of Manasseh, but could now
bring the Ark back into the newly cleansed Temple. Or it
might mean that the Ark had been taken in procession around
Jerusalem, or otherwise travelled with the Levites, and that
Josiah was not keen that the practice continued. But whatever it does mean, it means that the Ark existed and was in
Jerusalem or available to be restored to Jerusalem. And the
clear sense of the verse is that it was indeed restored to the
Temple.

And there, it seems, it remained; at least until the
Babylonian threat loomed large.

There was nothing sudden or surprising about the threat
from the north. In 722/721 BC the Northern Kingdom of
Israel had been engulfed by the Assyrians, and in 701 BC the
vast army of Sennacherib of Assyria had camped outside
Jerusalem, only to be struck down miraculously by an angel
of the Lord. The prophets of Jerusalem insisted that this was
only a respite, not a deliverance, and they were right.

The chronology of the eventual defeat and exile matters:
it indicates that anyone concerned to ensure that the crucial
treasures of Israel were safe had plenty of time to prepare.

Jehoiakim, King of Judah (c. 609–598 BC), became a vassal of Nebuchadnezzar of Babylon. He rebelled against
Babylon, was apparently killed, and was succeeded by his son

Jehoiachin. Nebuchadnezzar besieged Jerusalem and took it in March 597 BC, taking Jehoiachin prisoner and carrying him off to Babylon, along with the soldiers, artisans and officials of Jerusalem. 'No one remained, except the poorest people of the land...' Nebuchadnezzar 'carried off all the treasures of the house of the Lord, and the treasures of the king's house; he cut in pieces all the vessels of gold in the temple of the Lord, which King Solomon of Israel had made...' Nebuchadnezzar put Jehoiachin's uncle on the throne, changing his name to Zedekiah.

Was the Ark included in the spoils, or destroyed? In the absence of a specific mention of the Ark, it seems highly unlikely.

This was not the end of the First Temple. That came later. Zedekiah sought an alliance with Egypt, and rebelled against Nebuchadnezzar's rule. The result was predictably disastrous. The siege of Jerusalem began in January 587 BC. It lasted eighteen months. In July 586 the walls were breached. Zedekiah, who had managed to escape, was caught in the plains of Jericho. The last thing that he saw before the Babylonians put out his eyes was the death of his sons.

The rape of Jerusalem was brutal and diligent. Nebuzaradan, the captain of the bodyguard, 'burned the house of the Lord, the king's house and all the houses of Jerusalem; every great house he burned down. All the army of the Chaldeans who were with the captain of the guard broke down the walls around Jerusalem...' Zedekiah was carried off to Babylon, along with most of the remaining population. There, by the waters of Babylon, they did their best to sing the Lord's song in a strange land.

And this is where the speculation begins. The Bible last

spoke of the Ark as it was being restored to its rightful place in the Temple under King Josiah; it never says again that the Ark is in Jerusalem. Jewish tradition is clear: the Ark was not in the Second Temple, built by the returning Jerusalemites after the 529 BC edict of Cyrus of Persia let them go. Tacitus agrees: when the Roman general Pompey stalked blasphemously into the Holy of Holies in AD 63, it was empty.

If you manage to survive the homicidal Roman traffic and walk up the Via Sacra to the Victory Arch commemorating the sack of the Temple in AD 70, you will see many Temple artefacts on it, including a characteristic menorah; but there is no sign of the greatest prize of all – the Ark. Titus was not a man to blush self-deprecatingly and fail to mention a grand achievement. So when the former Benedictine monk, Nelson Comode, now of Texas, told the world that he had been taken to a secret cave beneath the monastery at Subiaco, near Rome, and there shown Temple treasures, including the Ark and the Tabernacle, he was displaying depressing historical illiteracy. He had not read his Tacitus. Some of the Jewish treasures looted by Titus have no doubt found their way into Vatican treasuries. But the Ark was not amongst them: it was long gone.

So where did it go?

Did it go to Babylon as spoils of war? That is certainly what the apocryphal book, 2 Esdras, supported by the Talmud Babli, says. But it seems unlikely. Both 2 Esdras and the Talmud Babli need to be treated with great caution. The relevant part of 2 Esdras is confidently dated to the last decade of the first century AD, and the relevant part of the Talmud to somewhere between the third and seventh centuries AD. They are both engaging in clear *ex post facto* reconstruction, and do not purport to rely on any primary or near-primary resources. The canonical Bible has a detailed inventory of what the Babylonians took, and the Ark is not on it. For what it is worth, Eupolemus, a Jewish historian writing in the second century BC, notes the tribute that was taken off to Babylon, and says specifically that the Ark and the tablets were not with it. The Book of Ezra also asserts that the Temple vessels that were taken were kept and returned to Jerusalem with the returning exiles. If vessels were kept and returned, surely the Ark itself would have been returned had it been taken. And if it had been taken and not returned, surely Ezra would have had something to say about it.

Was it destroyed with the Temple? Again, this seems unlikely. It was covered in gold. And again, if it had been, one might expect some sort of explicit scriptural wailing. There is nothing.

So perhaps the Ark survived. But how? And where?

Some say that it was hidden – presumably by men in the High Priest's circle – and the secret of its whereabouts lost when the men in the know were killed by the Babylonians. This would not be surprising: the Babylonians were notoriously rough. It would also explain why, when the exiles returned from Babylon, the Ark was not brought out of its hiding-place, dusted off, and restored to the rebuilt Temple. But there are other good explanations for its non-restoration. After the decree of Cyrus, Jerusalem was always a precarious place; always looking nervously over its shoulder, waiting for the next violation. It had been taught traumatically, over many centuries, just how vulnerable the Ark was. If the keepers of the secret survived Nebuchadnezzar, they could be forgiven for deciding that the Ark was too precious and

too envied to be placed within the reach of the next Middle
Eastern superpower. Their judgment was amply vindicated
by the behaviour of the Greeks and the Romans.

Ark-hunting is big business. The internet seethes with dis-
cussion of the Ark's whereabouts. Cryptic references in
ancient texts are the launching pads for wild speculation. A
mention in the Mishnayot of Rabbi Hertz (supposedly written in Babylon during the captivity) of a 'desolate valley
under a hill – on its east side, forty stones deep' becomes for
some the Tomb of Tutankhamun. If that's right, then thousands of overheated tourists file unknowingly past the Ark
every day at the Egyptian Museum, spared the penalty of the
men of Beth Shemesh. If you're a Mormon with an excitable
disposition, the Ark is in the Sanpete Valley, in the outskirts
of Utah, lugged over there by Lehi. If you're a loyal Japanese
citizen with a taste for sci-fi, the Ark is on Mount Tsurugizan
on Shikoku Island.

For the English writer Graham Phillips, the Ark was, and
presumably still is, in a field between Banbury and Coventry
in the English Midlands. And indeed, he has found one of the
Tablets of the Law. For him, Mount Sinai is Jebel Madhbah,
an echoing sandstone wall at Petra. The Arab chronicler
Numairi, writing about AD 1300, spoke about some Western
knights discovering, in the 1180s, a sealed cave at the mountain, inside which were 'treasures of pure gold, precious
stones, and a golden chest'. This chest, thinks Phillips, was
the Ark of the Covenant, and those knights were Templars.
Amongst the treasure were the 'Stones of Fire' from the
High Priest's breastplate. Phillips claims to have found some
of these stones in England, and says that they were used to
control the power of the Ark, and to protect the wearer from

it. Look at what happens to unprotected people, he says: ask Aaron's sons, or the pitiful Uzzah.

He thinks that the Templars who found the Ark at Petra came from Temple Herdewyke in Warwickshire. They would have known about some strange lights that were often then and are often now seen floating over the Burton Dassett hills – often taken for ghosts or UFOs. Those lights, thinks Phillips, were generated by geoplasma, and are perhaps a consequence of the peculiar geology of the Burton Dassett hills. Having discovered the Ark, the Templars would have found that its power was geoplasmic, and no doubt would have seen it generate and attract phenomena similar to the ones they knew from Warwickshire. The Templars would have thought that this was a sign that they should take the Ark back with them. To take it to Warwickshire would be taking the Ark to visit its family.

In the fourteenth century the Black Death wiped out the descendants of these Templars, but not before they had managed to hide, encrypted in some curious paintings on the wall of Burton Dassett church, the clues to the hiding-place of the Ark. Phillips and some American friends followed the clues to an ancient holy well in the Warwickshire village of Napton-on-the-Hill.

We went there too, one grey January day when the rooks were muttering away in the swaying elms of Napton. A monosyllabic newsagent had to direct us. It was a stinking pond, bordered by some of the overheated brick houses with integral garages that you get if you work hard in human resources in Birmingham. Once it had been a holy well, visited by pilgrims and healers, and fed by a stream that rose high up on the border with Oxfordshire. The well had been smashed up by roadworks in the 1940s. In the bank of the stream one of Phillips' party found a sandstone slab, about a foot and a half long, a foot wide and an inch thick, deeply inscribed with thirteen archaic symbols which have so far defied the translators. This, Phillips thinks, might be one of the Tablets of the Law. It is apparently in the USA at the moment, being analysed. 'Well, I'm not convinced,' said my wife Mary, who had stayed in the car eating a pork pie and reading a Lakeland Plastics catalogue. And that's the general view.

But Phillips and his ilk are eccentrics in the Ark-hunting world. Most Ark-hunters think that the trail starts getting hot in Jerusalem, and many think that it never leaves there.

There is one name that keeps cropping up in documents relating to the fate of the Ark. That name is Jeremiah. Eupolemus, for instance, whom we've met already, says that Jeremiah preserved the Ark and the Tablets. On the face of it, Jeremiah is a likely repository for the secrets of the Ark. He was a descendant of Abiathar, one of King David's chief priests, and would have been well connected to the ecclesiastical hierarchy of the Temple. After the destruction of Jerusalem, Jeremiah decided to stay behind in the city to help to pick up the pieces. Perhaps he had another agenda in staying behind. Eventually he was forced into exile in Egypt, and is never heard of again in the pages of the canonical scriptures.

The final Old Testament reference to the historical Ark (there are references which aren't intended to give information about the physical Ark, such as passages in Ezekiel, where the Ark appears in apocalyptic visions) is in the Book of Jeremiah. It gives no details of where the Ark is; it is cryptic, mysterious and highly and hotly discussed. It is early in the book, and it purports to be purely prophetic in nature and to come from, or from near to, the time of Jeremiah's call to prophetic ministry in 627 BC – the thirteenth year of King Josiah's reign. It was purportedly written, therefore, long before the first exile to Babylon in 597 and the destruction of Jerusalem in 586.

> I will give you shepherds after my own heart, who will feed you with knowledge and understanding. And when you have multiplied and increased in the land, in those days, says the Lord, they shall no longer say, 'The Ark of the Covenant of the Lord.' It shall not come to mind, or be remembered, or missed; nor shall another one be made. At that time Jerusalem shall be called the throne of the Lord, and all nations shall gather to it, to the presence of the Lord in Jerusalem, and they shall no longer stubbornly follow their own evil will…

On one level this seems to be straightforward enough: it is a prophecy of what in fact happened – that the Ark of the Covenant went missing from Jerusalem – together with a vision of a renewed, possibly Messianic Jerusalem. But the scriptural cryptographers have been hard at work. 'Look at "they shall no longer say…"' the argument goes. 'That clearly implies that at the time this was written, people were already saying that the Ark had gone missing. Perhaps it had gone with Shishak after all. Or perhaps Manasseh's blasphemy had been more profound than the Bible tells us; perhaps he had removed or destroyed the Ark. Perhaps the real agenda behind Josiah's downplaying of cultic Temple worship was that the Ark was not there any more.' Well, perhaps. But all these theories don't live comfortably with that curious but clear verse from the Second Book of Chronicles about the Ark being carried on Levitical shoulders.

If one leaves the canonical scriptures and goes to those under-read extra-canonical books that appear in some copies of the Bible, there is a clear account of what happened to the Ark. It is in the Second Book of Maccabees:

> It was also in the same document that the prophet [Jeremiah], having received an oracle, ordered that the tent and the Ark should follow with him, and that he went out to the mountain where Moses had gone up and had seen the inheritance of God [Mount Nebo]. Jeremiah came and found a cave-dwelling, and he brought there the tent and the Ark and the altar of incense; then he sealed up the entrance. Some of those who followed him came up intending to mark the way, but could not find it. When Jeremiah learned of it, he rebuked them and declared: 'The place shall remain unknown until God gathers his people together again and shows his mercy. Then the Lord will disclose these things, and the glory of the Lord and the cloud will appear, as they were shown in the case of Moses, and as Solomon asked that the place should be specially consecrated...'

The sources behind this account are unknown. The 'document' described has never been definitely identified, although we will meet some exotic suggestions. At any rate, this part of 2 Maccabees may have been written as early as 164 BC. Might it be true? Well, yes, it might. But it is as well to remember what the real agenda of this document is. It is to encourage Egyptian Jews who are having a hard time. It will all come right, the letter says: remember how God intervened in the heroic era of Judas Maccabaeus: he can do the same now. A crucial part of morale-maintenance for hard-pressed Jews was to believe that proper Temple worship, as in the halcyon Solomonic days, would one day be restored. And the Ark is a central part of that dream. This theme – back to the golden age – is in many of the other tales mentioning the Ark. In the Apocalypse of Baruch, Baruch sees an angel removing the Ark, along with the Temple vessels, before the Babylonian destruction. Hide them, the earth is ordered, until Jerusalem is redeemed. In 4 Baruch Jeremiah is told by God to bury the vessels until 'the Beloved One' comes. The Book of Enoch tells us that the Tabernacle is buried in some secret cache in the south, and will be uncovered when the Messiah inaugurates a new age. In the medieval Jewish *Sepher Yosippon*, Elijah and Jeremiah together reveal the hiding-place of the Ark. None of this stuff has the distinctive smell of history. Where the psychological agenda is so strong, historical credibility is correspondingly weaker. I wouldn't put money into an expedition to Mount Nebo on the back of these accounts.

But many have. There must be more metal detectors on Mount Nebo than on any other hill in the Middle East. In the 1920s the American explorer Antonia Frederick Futterer said that he had found an inscription which showed where on Mount Nebo the Ark was hidden. He did not excavate it himself. That job was left to another American, one Tom Crotser, who went to Jordan in 1981 with three friends and Futterer's sketch, and claimed to have found the cave that Maccabees speaks of. He had no licence to excavate, but that didn't stop him burrowing through a stone wall into a chamber. And there he found a gold-covered box and some gauze-wrapped objects which he took to be the cherubim. The party did not touch the artefacts, found a disappointing and surprising lack of interest in the authorities to whom they went with news of this epic find, and went back to America. The story was written up for a US newspaper, but without the colour pictures that Crotser had taken. Crotser was cautious about showing his pictures, but he made the mistake of showing them to an eminent archaeologist, Siegfried Horn. All the slides were of poor quality, Horn reported: only two showed anything at all. One of these showed a chamber with a yellowish box. The other showed the front of the box. The metal was plainly machined, said Horn, and the photograph clearly showed a nail with a modern head. Horn dismissed the story as a hoax, and it has not raised its head much since.

Others think that the reference is actually to the mountains on the Israeli side of the Dead Sea – to the area of Qumran, where the Dead Sea Scrolls were found. Foremost amongst them is the colourful Texan, Vendyl Jones. And behind his life and work is the story of another strange object – the Copper Scroll.

I shudder whenever I go to Qumran. It is not with the cold, for it is never cold, even when the snow lies thick in Jerusalem, twenty miles away. It is because it is a haunted place, where the shades and the wadis and the ages press close. The tour-buses of loud New York college kids come to find their inheritance don't exorcise the place; nor does the air-conditioned gift shop where you can buy Dead Sea mud face-packs and over-priced nylon camels; nor do the vicious academic debates about what this place was. Perhaps it was a pottery. Or perhaps it was the headquarters of the Essenes, devoted to making, away from the terminally compromised world of Second Temple Judaism, a place pure enough to welcome the Messiah. Whatever it was, its dead are the most vocal and articulate of Israel.

The kids don't bother to shamble, chewing, beyond the well-signposted ruins just inside the site entrance. If they went a few steps they would be able to see the cave into which, in 1947, a shepherd boy flung a stone. He heard the clink of a breaking pot, and climbed up to find the scrolls that revolutionized biblical scholarship. These were the Dead Sea Scrolls, and they are no concern of ours, except that they brought some serious archaeologists to Qumran. And in 1952 those archaeologists found, at the back of Cave 3, two copper rolls.

They were badly corroded, and could not simply be unrolled. They were cut into strips, and it became clear that they were part of the same document. It is a listing of treasure trove. Sixty-four locations are listed: sixty-three describe the hiding-places of gold or silver. The descriptions given are arcane and difficult to follow: they evidently imply a very detailed knowledge of some area, and the caches they describe seem to have been elaborately constructed.

Academic opinion is hotly divided about the Copper Scroll. Some think that it is an elaborate hoax, and that the people responsible must be laughing themselves silly at the reverence and expense lavished on the treasure hunt. Of those who take the Scroll seriously, some think that it describes Essene treasure (which is slightly odd, if the Essenes were world-renouncing ascetics), some Second Temple treasure, and some the treasure of the First Temple.

Vendyl Jones has no doubt. Since 1968 he has been trying to follow the clues of the Scroll, which he is clear describes the location of the First Temple treasures. He claims two major successes, which he says vindicate the Scroll and his reading of it. In 1988 he found a small jug of thick oil. This, he says, was the Holy Anointing Oil from the First Temple. And in 1992 his team uncovered a hidden silo in the bedrock containing over 900 pounds of a reddish snuff-like material. He claims that analysis showed this to be a compound of eleven of the ingredients of the Temple's holy incense. Both these items are listed in the Copper Scroll, which Jones thinks is one of the missing documents referred to in the Second Book of Maccabees.

Jones has his eye on bigger trophies than oil and dust, whether sacred or not. The Copper Scroll says this:

> In the desolations of the Valley of Achor, under the hill that must be climbed, hidden under the east side, forty stones deep, is a silver chest; and with it the vestments of the High Priest, all the gold and silver with the Great Tabernacle and all its treasures.

It goes further, saying that these objects are in 'The Cave of the Column'.

The chest, says Jones, is the Ark itself. He believes that he has located the Cave of the Column, and says that the Cave is linked by a passage to the Temple Mount in Jerusalem. It was through this passage, he says, that King Zedekiah made his way out of Jerusalem towards the plains of Jericho during the Babylonian siege. Jones believes that he is not far from the Ark, and is palpably frustrated at the limitations on his excavation imposed by economics and Israeli bureaucracy.

The archaeological establishment has, by and large, been roundly dismissive of Jones' claims. Talking about the 'incense', a leading archaeologist told me that 'He found a load of simple, straightforward Judean dust'.

The strangest part of the Jeremiah trail leads a very long way from Jerusalem.

The plane was wretchedly late, and as it churned through black cloud and skimmed over hedges built for hunting, a child vomited. But for all that, I was very glad to be back in Ireland. I can easily forgive, on the grounds that the English have a lot of forgiving to do to the Irish, the cynicism of the pervasive leprechaun culture and the bogus Oyrish chain pubs with their absurd lumps of peat and sepia pictures of New York drama students dressed like plaintive Kerry milk-maids. We hired a small and hysterically overpriced car and drove to some place where, improbably, it was raining even harder than at the airport. We remortgaged our house to buy a bag of chips, and then fell asleep to the sound of a cat-fight.

We woke in pouring rain and drove in pouring rain to a place in the Royal County of Meath where it was raining a lot. 'It's wet,' said Mary, and it was. We sat in a café drinking tea, waiting for it to clear up, and sniggering at the naivety of the tourists who were paying huge prices for the guidebooks. Then we found that we had left ours in London, bought one ourselves, and went out into the heavy drizzle that the Irish call sunshine to get on with the day.

We were here because it has been repeatedly suggested with a straight face and footnotes that the Prophet Jeremiah brought the Ark of the Covenant here, possibly via Spain, and buried it on the Hill of Tara – the ancient capital of the kings of Ireland. What is there now, on the top of a small but sur-prisingly commanding hill, is a series of complex earth-

works, a Bronze Age passage-grave known as Dumha na
nGiall – the Mound of the Hostages – and the Lia Fail, the
inauguration stone of the kings of Tara, which roars when
touched by the anointed king. The dates are important for
our purposes: the Mound of the Hostages probably dates to
around 2100 BC; the main earthworks are probably from the
first to the fifth centuries AD.

At the end of the nineteenth century a group of Ark-
seekers came to Tara and started to dig. They were so-called
'British Israelites' who believed that the British were the
Chosen People to whom the baton of David and Solomon had
been solemnly handed. One of the crucial pieces of evidence
of British chosenness was that the Prophet Jeremiah had
buried the Ark at Tara. It would have been less politically
ambiguous if he had chosen to bury it at Tunbridge Wells,
but no, Tara is where it is, they said. It's not clear to me why
they chose Tara, and it doesn't seem to have been particularly
clear to them either. They didn't find it, of course, but they
did make a mighty mess of the so-called Rath of the Synods,
where Saints Patrick, Brendan, Ruadhan and Adamnan are
said to have had a summit conference. Subsequent excavations of the Rath showed that the history of the site extended
from the first to the third centuries AD. There was no hint of
anything earlier.

There are some modern mutations of the Irish Jeremiah
story doing the rounds on the internet. One of the most vig-
orously peddled ones, accompanied by some of the most
explicit reasoning, dives deep into the collection of ancient
Irish legends known as the Dinnshenchas.

First there is the matter of Tara's name. There is an old
and persistent story that it was named after a lady of great

wisdom and beauty called Teia. She, according to the Dinnshenchas, was of Milesian origin, having come originally from Spain. Now she, say the internet enthusiasts, was the daughter of King Zedekiah of Jerusalem, and Jeremiah had been commissioned by God to maintain the royal line through her. So after the destruction of Jerusalem, Teia went with Jeremiah, the scribe Baruch and the Ark of the Covenant (previously hidden from Babylonian eyes under the Temple Mount) to Tanis in Egypt, then to Gibraltar (hence the Spanish flavour in the Teia stories), and (losing Baruch on the way) eventually to Ireland, where Teia preserved the line of Zedekiah by marrying Eochaidh mac Duach, High King of Ireland, on 21 June 583 BC.

The metrical Dinnshenchas say that the resting-place of Teia was a mound sixty feet in diameter. That, say the Jeremiah theorists, has to be the Mound of the Hostages at Tara. There are two final links to the Ark of the Covenant: Teia, according to the Dinnshenchas, was 'the secret place of the Way of Life'. And what is the 'Way of Life' according to the Bible? Answer: the law of Moses, as recorded on the tablets in the Ark. So the Ark is just there for the taking, a few feet down beneath one of the most visited monuments in Ireland, served not by Levites but by a visitors' centre and a knitwear shop. But the Jeremiah connection is said to be even stronger than that.

We drove as fast as we could, because it was a late-autumn afternoon and the light was fading. Small roads gave way to tracks bounded by high blackthorn hedges, a herd of cattle on its way to milking wound slowly before us into a farm, and we climbed. Climbed out of the rolling dairy-land of Meath into a new country: a high, brooding country of sheep and crows, close to the clouds, where stone breaks out of the grass like bones. We parked up at the foot of the highest hill: Shiabh na Caillighe, the Hill of the Witch. A shepherd, leaning on a gate, said that it was late to be going all the way up there. But it wasn't far. The path lies in a wedge between the hill and a gaunt hedge, writhing with ivy. There was a sentinel crow at every twist of the path, and as we walked up they all peeled off to the summit.

These were the Loughcrew 'Passage Tombs'. They are all on the hill-top, in a position that a boy and a dog could hold against an army. And it is in the biggest of these, Cairn T, that some say the Prophet Jeremiah himself is buried.

The evidence for this is said to lie in some very curious and elaborate hieroglyphics carved on a stone inside the entrance to the tomb. These are supposed to tell the story of Jeremiah's and Teia's journey to Ireland, changing from a Tyrian to a Greek boat at Gibraltar. In the last of the day's thin storm-light we could just make out the cryptic swirls on the stone. Walking up the other side of the hill was a man in a dark cowl. 'It's perfect,' said Mary. 'I do hope it's true.'

But unfortunately there is no serious possibility that the Mound of the Hostages and the Cairn T theories are right. The dates are miles out. The Milesians of the Dinnshenchas, if they really existed, were hugely more ancient than a biblical Teia would have been. They are said to have come from Spain in 1700 BC. The Mound of the Hostages has been exhaustively excavated. No Ark was found, but about forty Middle Bronze Age burials were. They have been confidently dated to the middle of the second millennium BC. Carbon 14 methods have dated the mound itself, and its surrounding ditch, to about 2000 BC.

The Loughcrew dates are even further from the mark. The tombs (if they are tombs at all) were built in the Neolithic period, by the first farmers of Ireland. The stone markings at Cairn T seem to be some sort of astronomical calculator. At dawn on the days of the Spring and Autumn equinox, sunlight enters the tomb and illuminates the carvings. The carvings thus seem to have been present at the time of the construction of the tomb: they weren't added later to tell the tale of a Prophet who had travelled with a Lady and an Ark to graft the bloodline of the kings of Jerusalem into Ireland.

The most persistent rumours about the Ark, though, say that it was hidden in Jerusalem itself at or around the time of the Babylonian conquest. Some of these stories involve Jeremiah; some do not. The most dramatic involves our friend Ron Wyatt.

We left him in Chapter 2, having triumphantly discovered the site of Mount Sinai. But before that, of course, he had been diving in the Gulf of Aqaba and finding the wheels of Pharaoh's chariots. In 1978, when he was out diving, his legs and feet became so sunburned that he couldn't get his fins on. He was forced to abandon the trip and to return to Jerusalem. He decided to go sightseeing in the area near his hotel, just next to Damascus Gate. He was walking along near the old Arab bus station, chatting to a friend about Roman antiquities. Then something very strange happened. Wyatt's wife, Mary Nell, tells the story:

'At one point they stopped walking, and Ron's left hand pointed to a site being used as a trash dump and he stated, "That's Jeremiah's Grotto and the Ark of the Covenant is in there." Even though these words had come from his own mouth and his own hand had pointed, he had not consciously done or said these things. In fact it was the first time he had ever thought about excavating for the Ark.'

The man he was walking with said immediately, and apparently quite out of character: 'That's wonderful! We want you to excavate, and we'll furnish your permits, put you up in a place to stay, and even furnish your meals!' So in January 1979 Wyatt and his sons returned to Jerusalem and began digging in a part of the Garden Tomb complex, just in front of the cliff which forms part of the escarpment into which the Tomb itself is cut.

The Garden Tomb is a wonderful place; a resonant oasis of calm and cool, beautifully maintained by an English Trust, where prayer comes a lot more easily than in the sectarian buzz of the Church of the Holy Sepulchre. It is next to a skull-shaped hill that General Gordon thought must be the hill of Calvary, and many Protestants believe that the tomb found in the garden is the tomb of Joseph of Arimathea in which Jesus was laid and from which he rose. I wish that they were right, but they're not. The informed archaeological consensus is complete: the tomb is a typical seventh- or eighth-century BC tomb which forms part of the First Temple period northern cemetery. It was reused in Byzantine times, but was certainly not a 'new tomb' at the time of Jesus, as demanded by the New Testament. There are no Second Temple period tombs at all in the area.

Anyway, Ron Wyatt – a man whose opinions were always blissfully unencumbered by the facts – was a firm believer in the historicity of the Garden Tomb. When they started digging, 'almost immediately' (those words again), he found a niche cut into the face of the cliff. A little further down he found two more. He was convinced that they had been cut to hold the signs placed over the cross of Jesus in Hebrew, Greek and Latin, announcing that this was 'Jesus of Nazareth, the King of the Jews'. He dug further down, finding a hole that he decided had held the cross itself. And from this hole, a crack, plainly caused by the earthquake spoken of by St Matthew, extended down into the bedrock. It was not until 1982 that he found what the crack led to.

Wyatt and his sons, helped by a young Arab they called 'James', explored many of the narrow tunnels inside the escarpment. On 6 January 1982 Wyatt and 'James' found a very small opening in the wall of the tunnel they were in. Looking through it with his flashlight, Wyatt could see nothing but a chamber full of rocks, with about eighteen inches of clearance between the rocks and the ceiling. Although it looked unpromising, they enlarged the opening, and 'James' crawled in.

> Almost as soon as 'James' crawled through the tiny opening, he frantically came tumbling back out, shaking and shouting 'What's in there? What's in there? I'm not going back in there!!' Ron saw in his eyes sheer, complete and utter terror – yet James said that he had seen nothing! But whatever he experienced was real, for he left not only that chamber, but the entire cave system, never to return.

Left alone, Wyatt decided that he had to investigate. He enlarged the hole and wriggled in. Seeing something shiny, he saw some rotted animal skins covering a gold-veneered table that he was later to conclude was the Table of Shewbread from the First Temple. He shone his flashlight around, and up to the ceiling. If his account is accurate, what he saw next was easily the most momentous discovery of all time:

> ...it was a crack in the ceiling with a black substance within the crack. Crawling slowly and painfully over the rocks to the rear of the chamber, he saw a stone case extending through the rocks. It had a flat stone top which was cracked completely in two and the smaller section was moved aside, creating an opening into the stone case. But the top was too near the ceiling for him to look inside. Yet he knew what was inside – the crack in the ceiling was directly above the cracked part of the lid, where it was open, and the black substance had fallen from the crack into the case because some of it had splashed onto the lid. It was at this time, as Ron recalls, as the instant realization of what had happened here dawned on him, that he passed out. When he realized that the crack in the ceiling was the end of the crack he had found in the elevated cross-hole many feet above him, and the black substance was blood which had fallen through the crack and into the stone case, he KNEW the Ark was in the stone case. But the most overwhelming realization was that Christ's blood had actually fallen onto the Mercy Seat. [Original emphasis.]

Wyatt remained unconscious for forty-five minutes. When he came to he climbed out through the small hole, went back through the series of tunnels, and sealed the passageway with a stone. He could see no way of removing anything from the chamber where he had seen the Ark.

He returned to the chamber 'on several occasions'. On one occasion he took a drill, managed to bore a hole in the stone case, and peered inside using a colonoscope:

> ...he guided [the colonoscope] downward, rotating the lens until he saw what he recognised as the bottom of the crown-moulding around the top of the Mercy Seat, and then he saw the flat golden side. Since the colonoscope doesn't allow viewing of a large area, and since he had little means to guide it other than a small latitude of rotation, he couldn't see a great deal. But he saw enough to KNOW it was the Ark. [Original emphasis.]

He said that he knew that the stone tablets were inside the Ark: it is not clear, given his limited view, how he knew this.

Alongside the Ark in the chamber, together with other objects that Wyatt was unable to identify, were the Table of Shewbread that he had seen first, the Golden Altar of Incense, the Golden Censer, the seven-branched Menorah (which apparently had tiny oil lamps instead of candles), a huge sword, an ephod, a mitre with an ivory pomegranate, a brass shekel weight, many oil lamps and a brass ring. All these objects were covered with dry-rotted animal skins. Rotted wooden timbers were on top of the skins, and rocks were piled over everything. Unfortunately none of his photos came out.

Wyatt's most outlandish claim ever related to the 'blood' he said was on the Mercy Seat. He said that he had got it analysed. The chromosomes, after all those years, were still visible. And they were very peculiar. In normal human cells there are forty-six chromosomes. Half come from the father, and half from the mother. But this blood had twenty-four chromosomes. Twenty-three were from Jesus' mother Mary, it was claimed; the other one was a 'Y' chromosome, which could only have come from God. It was scientific proof of the divinity of Jesus. The results have never been provided.

Wyatt continued to excavate. He apparently presumed that all the artefacts had been carried into the chambers through another entrance, which he hoped to find. He also believed that there must be a tunnel running from the Temple Mount to the chamber, through which the objects had been smuggled away during the Babylonian siege. He found neither, and was getting disillusioned when he heard a voice behind him saying, 'God bless you in what you are doing here.' He looked up to see 'a tall, slender man with dark hair wearing a long, white robe and head covering similar to that worn in Biblical times – except that it was all pure white.' Wyatt tried to make conversation, but the man replied monosyllabically, and finally said: 'I'm on my way from South Africa to the New Jerusalem.' Wyatt was startled into silence. The stranger repeated his original blessing and walked away. No one had seen the man enter or leave, or recognized his description. Wyatt believed that he had seen Jesus himself, and was hugely encouraged.

Wyatt died in 1999, but his disciples at Wyatt Archaeological Research continued to believe that he had been telling the truth about the Ark. Money flowed in to finance the excavation. Sophisticated ground-penetrating radar was deployed. But the mysterious chamber was never relocated. And then, in 2005, scepticism seemed to grow, even amongst the inner circle of the true believers. The 'cross-hole' was uncovered, and it was conclusively demonstrated that there was no crack extending downwards from it. Wyatt Archaeological Research would not say that Wyatt had lied, choosing instead to put out a statement saying: '…at this time it is important to state…that Ron's account of his discovery of the Ark of the Covenant cannot be con-

firmed and that recent exploration reveals unexplained discrepancies in that account...' They have removed from their
website all of Wyatt's original account of the 'discovery'.

But evidence often doesn't have a lot to do with belief.
Indeed, the strength of a belief is often inversely propor-
tional to the strength of the evidence. And so, of course,
there is a hard core of immovably faithful Wyatt-ists – mostly
Seventh Day Adventists – who continue to pour money, time
and no doubt prayer into this plainly absurd investigation.

Surprisingly few people say that Ron Wyatt was lying. He
came over even to his most virulent opponents – of whom
my great friend Joe Zias, doyen of Israeli forensic archaeologists, is proud to be the chief – as a straightforward person
who appeared to believe what he said. That was certainly the
opinion of Peter Wells, the Administrator of the Garden
Tomb. I've known him for years, and like him very much.
He's the most genial of men, but he was distinctly uneasy
when I confronted him in the Garden and asked about Ron
Wyatt. And no wonder. It's plainly embarrassing for the
Garden Tomb Association to have countenanced Ron Wyatt's
obsession with the Ark of the Covenant. Wyatt's lasting
legacy is to have made Christianity seem ridiculous and
Christians seem pathologically credulous.

There are plenty of reasons for doubting Ron Wyatt. If
any other reason is needed, it is the intrinsic improbability of
the location he dug in. Vendyl Jones at least has the Copper
Scroll. The Ethiopian theorists at least have the *Kebra Nagast*
and the curious customs of the Falashas. Ron Wyatt had nothing whatever apart from his supernaturally raised arm. A
location in the area of the Damascus Gate, where the
Babylonian siege would have been particularly dense, is pecu-
liarly unlikely.

The most persistent of the rumours points far nearer the Ark's own home: to the Temple Mount itself. And indeed, if you believe what you read in the newspapers, the Ark, along with other treasure from Solomon's Temple, was found there in 1911. It is a very strange story indeed.

Jerusalem had a simple but devastating problem with its water supply: how could a city on a hill get water from a neighbouring valley when it is surrounded by a besieging army? The problem was solved with extraordinary ingenuity by the systems now known as Warren's Shaft and Hezekiah's Tunnel. In the early twentieth century a Finnish surveyor, poet and biblical historian called Valter Henrik Juvelius pored over the plans of this system, linked them with a code which he thought he could see in the Book of Ezekiel, and decided that the available plans did not tell the whole story: there were other covert tunnels leading up from the ancient water system into the Temple Mount itself. These tunnels, he believed, led to the Ark of the Covenant and the treasure of Solomon.

We do not know what his Ezekiel Code was: the secret died with him. But it is not ridiculous to link Ezekiel with the hiding-place of the Ark. Ezekiel was a priest and the son of a priest, and he was exiled to Babylon, where he probably died. If the Ark was hidden by someone in the Jerusalem priestly hierarchy, he was the sort of person who might have known where it was.

Dangling the carrot of unimaginable riches and immortal fame before their noses, Juvelius persuaded a group of European adventurers to finance an expedition to recover the Ark. Apart from Juvelius and a Swedish engineer called

Millen, they were all English nobles. Prominent amongst them was Captain Montague Parker, a Duke's son.

In August 1909, brandishing an excavation permit from the Ottoman government (obtained by promising the government half of the treasure found), the expedition arrived in Jerusalem and started to dig in the area of the Gihon spring.

The details of the expedition are hard to piece together: there are radically divergent accounts. But it seems that it began by everyone following Juvelius' Code. If you believe Millen, they continued to follow it, being reassured by the discovery of Solomonic artefacts, until they had nearly reached the Ark. Parker's account is different. He realized that the clues in the Code were leading the excavation away from the Temple Mount, and seems to have taken the opportunity, when Juvelius fell ill and returned to Finland in the autumn of 1910, to take matters into his own hands.

In April 1911 the Muslim festival of Nebi Musa, the Greek Orthodox Easter and the Jewish Passover all fell together. Parker saw his chance. He thought that while Jerusalem was drunk with religious ardour, he might have a clear run at the Temple Mount. For the massive sum of $25,000 (a good index of his confidence that there was something significant to be found), he bribed the Sheikh in charge of the Temple Mount. For the week the Sheikh would turn a blind eye to the excavation.

Parker and his men, dressed as Arabs, excavated by night beneath the Sakhra in the Dome of the Rock, and in 'Solomon's Stables' – a great underground area which has nothing to do with Solomon, where the Templars stabled their warhorses. The excavations went well. On the final night they were confident that they were about to break through to the Ark. But it all went terribly wrong. Parker had not bribed thoroughly enough. One of the custodians of the Dome of the Rock, asleep on the Temple Mount, was woken by the noise of the tunnelling. He raised the alarm, and immediately the streets of the Arab Quarter were full of angry crowds, baying for the blood of the infidel who had defiled the holy place of Islam.

Parker bolted for the port of Jaffa, but the telegraphed account of his illegal excavation got there first, and when he arrived he was arrested on charges of stealing the Ark of the Covenant, Mohammed's sword and Solomon's crown and ring. The arrest and the charges were duly reported, but the ever-resourceful Parker slipped through the net and managed to leave the country. Was the Ark on the boat with him? He never said so, and it seems unlikely. But there are millions of people who believe that he was not far from it on that night in April 1911.

I walked down through the Jewish Quarter of Jerusalem's Old City, past the falafel stores and the Judaica merchants, past a seven-year-old boy sitting on a wall reading Leviticus in Hebrew, his Playstation forgotten on his knee. On a side street is a curious and earnest museum. It is full of the Treasures of the Temple, all made, at vast expense, to the biblical and talmudic blueprint. It is not just a museum. These incense burners and candlesticks and washbowls are meant to be used in the Third Temple that the black-coated custodians believe will rise on the Temple Mount. There is one striking omission from the exhibits: there is no Ark of the Covenant. 'Of course not,' said the young man at the door, in a strong Brooklyn accent. 'Why build a replica when you can have the real thing?'

During Second Temple times, the Mishnah says, a priest was in the Temple Mount woodshed, collecting wood for the altar. He noticed something odd: one flagstone was higher than the others. This, the priest thought, must be where the Ark is hidden. He rushed to tell the other priests about his discovery, but fell dead in the middle of a sentence.

Some have always known the secret. The priests used to bow at thirteen places in the Second Temple, but a close observer would see that the house of Rabbis Gamaliel and Hananiah bowed at a fourteenth — towards the woodshed.

Mainstream Jewish tradition has been consistent about the location of the Ark. It is stored, together with the tablets, the Tabernacle, the altar of incense, the pot of manna and Aaron's rod in a compartment under the woodshed on the west side of the Temple, very close to the Holy of Holies. When the Temple was built, Solomon foresaw that the Temple itself would be endangered, and so built subterranean crypts in which to hide its treasures. 'There was a stone in the Holy of Holies, at its western wall, upon which the Ark rested,' wrote Maimonides in the twelfth century AD, summarizing the legends. 'In front of it stood the jar of manna and the staff of Aaron. When Solomon built the Temple, knowing that it was destined to be destroyed, he built underneath, in deep and winding tunnels, a place in which to hide the Ark. It was King Josiah who commanded the Ark be hidden in the place which Solomon had prepared.'

The Templars no doubt heard whispers of these stories. There is every reason to believe that they did conduct excavations under the Temple Mount, but none to think that they found the Ark. Assertions that they carried it off and that it is the mystery encoded in the Masonic cathedral of Rosslyn Chapel, the explanation for the enrichment of the corrupt, mass-trafficking priest Berenger Sauniere at Rennes le Chateau, or the reason for the orientation of Bornholm Chapel, shivering in the Danish Baltic, are just that — assertions. They have no evidential basis at all.

Archaeology does not contradict the ancient Jewish stories. For obvious political reasons there has been little modern scientific excavation of the Temple Mount. When Israeli paratroopers fought their way to the Western Wall in the Six Day War of 1967, it was hoped that a new archaeological era, if not the Messianic Age, was beginning. But it was not to be. After a month Israel relinquished control of the Temple Mount to the Muslim authorities, and the dream was postponed. But it is perfectly possible, as the Talmud insists, that Neburazadan left the foundational pavement of the Temple Mount intact, and therefore everything below that pavement intact.

In July 1981 Rabbi Shlomo Goren, the Chaplain of the Israeli Defence Forces who had briefly opened a synagogue on the Temple Mount in those heady days of 1967, received a late-night phone call from Rabbi Getz, who was Chief Rabbi of the Holy Places. Workmen clearing an area inside the Western Wall tunnel had uncovered one of the gates to the Temple Mount. This was not just any gate: it was the gate closest to the Holy of Holies, and was used by the priests for bringing in all the materials used in the Temple ceremonies. It was not a new discovery: the British engineer Charles Warren had found it in 1867, when the passage to which it led was being used as a cistern. (Warren was better at solving ancient mysteries than solving crimes. Later, as Commissioner of the Metropolitan Police, he signally failed to catch Jack the Ripper.)

Warren's excavation reports are odd. He was normally a careful, methodical man, but he was so unclear about the location of this particular tunnel that it was lost until another Briton, Charles Wilson, found it again, naming it 'Warren's Gate'. Warren was an active Freemason: it has been suggested that his curious obscurity was a consequence of his desire to keep the ancient secrets of the Temple out of the hands of non-members of the brotherhood.

Warren's Gate had been sealed. In the works of 1981 it was accidentally reopened. Rabbi Goren, according to the American writer Randall Price, swore to secrecy ten men, all of them religious Jews, and they began to clear the debris inside the tunnel in an attempt to reach the Ark. For more than a year and a half they worked at night. 'We were very close [to the Ark]', Rabbi Goren told an interviewer in 1991. 'We believe that the holy Ark made by Moses, and the table from the Temple, and the candelabra made by Moses, along with other very important items, are hidden very deep underneath the Holy of the Holies. We started digging and we came close to the place; we were not more than 30 or 40 yards away.'

But disaster struck. A reporter found out about the excavation and broadcast the information on the radio. Just as in the days of the Parker expedition, the Muslims of the Old City were enraged, and a mob attacked the excavation. Ariel Sharon, the then Defence Minister (later, and ironically, to cause such trouble himself by walking on the Temple Mount), refused to send any soldiers to help, and eventually a few hundred Yeshiva boys came to the rescue. They were only just in time.

The excavation was closed and a massive three-metre plug of steel and concrete was used to seal Warren's Gate. No one can get in from the Jewish-controlled Western Wall tunnels. Paranoid and unsubstantiated rumours perennially circulate about Arab efforts to find the Ark. But if nothing can get into where the Ark is, there is a persistent belief that something from the Ark gets out through the wall to the people outside.

It was my last night in Jerusalem. As always, departure felt like bereavement, although I am never quite sure what has died. As always, I went down to the Western Wall and sat there in the middle of that extraordinary holy hum. It was Shabbat evening, and the Yeshiva boys, newly washed and scrubbed, were processing down to the plaza to greet the Sabbath. 'Between right and left the Bride approaches,' they chanted, to a melody that had started in Babylon and been shaped in Poland. 'In holy jewels and festive garments. See, she comes.' When they reached the Wall some leapt and some bowed, and some clung to the Wall as if to a lover.

Clinging to and oozing from the stones of the Western Wall is the Shekhinah: the presence of God. The Shekhinah makes prophets prophesy, kings dance and joy illuminate the faces of children. It was with the Israelites as they journeyed through the wilderness, and filled the Temple when the Ark was brought in. And yet not 'it'. For the strangest thing of all is that Shekhinah is a feminine word. It is Judaism's very own expression of the sacred feminine, and it is right at the heart of the Jewish understanding of God. The songs of Jahweh and the Ark do not speak only of blood, thunder and massacre:

they are also, when the wind from the hills of Jerusalem is in the right direction, the songs of a mother to a child.

CHAPTER 10
Epilogue

If the storyteller is true to the story, in the end the silence
will speak. If the storyteller is not true to the story, in the
end there will be nothing but silence.

Karen Blixen

I have travelled thousands of miles in search of the Ark,
and have got no closer. This is very strange. As the journey progressed, I got more and more confused. I don't
know what the Ark is about, and I know less now than I ever
did. I have never met anyone who has got any *devotional*
mileage from the Ark. I have met plenty of people who
make, when I press them, the obvious speeches in the Ark's
favour: the Ark shows that God is a pilgrim God, guiding and
sojourning with his people. And so on. And their speeches
are fair enough. But the Bible takes you quickly from the
crossing of the Jordan to the buboes of the Philistine cities
and the tale of Uzzah, and there the speeches falter.

I have met, too, plenty of people who want the Ark
returned. But not for itself. They want the Messianic Age
that they think it will usher in. And if the Messianic Age is
Armageddon, they might well be right. If the Ark were

found, the impetus for the building of the Third Temple would become intense, and the world would be a much more dangerous place.

Whenever I think that I've understood the theology of the Ark, I go back to the Second Temple. Now what on earth or in heaven was going on there? Why were those thousands of oxen dying? What God was the blood of the turtle-doves appeasing? Where was he? It is plain that in the First Temple both the priests and the hoi polloi thought that he was sitting in or on a gold-covered box in the dark behind a curtain. And it is equally plain that in the Second Temple the box had gone. But had God gone too? There doesn't seem to have been any spectacular theological mutation when the Ark went missing. But why not? 'It would obviously be better if we had the Ark in the Third Temple,' said Jabo, as we drove through Samaria on the way back to Jerusalem from Shilo. 'In what sense would it be better?' I asked. But he just shrugged. Everyone always shrugs.

So I despair wholly of getting any systematic theology of the Ark. But that, now I come to think of it, is a conclusion worth reaching. My deepening incomprehension is something worth noting and worth having. The strangeness of growing bafflement in a world where immersion tends to mean familiarity is interesting and significant. I notice now that the Ark always evades its searchers. It slipped at the last minute out of the hands of Parker and Rabbi Goren. Wyatt saw it briefly, and then the rock slammed shut. Uzzah stretched out his hand, and his world closed up. The Ark is forever unreachable, and therefore desperately needed. It is transcendence incarnate.

Each step of this journey was a step into a new irony. And

here's the greatest. It's the story about God in a box that says that God won't go into a box. Which is some sort of comfort to anyone who hopes that he might operate outside one.

Select Bibliography

All biblical quotations are, unless otherwise stated, from the New Revised Standard Version.

The literature on the Ark and its whereabouts is immense. This bibliography contains a few of the hundreds of sources consulted in researching this book.

I. Ariel and C. Richman, *Carta's Illustrated Encyclopaedia of the Holy Temple in Jerusalem*, Jerusalem: Carta, 2006

A. Faust, *Israel's Ethnogenesis: Settlement, Interaction, Expansion and Resistance*, London: Equinox, 2007.

B. Feiler, *Walking the Bible*, London: Piatkus, 2001

I. Finkelstein and N. A. Silberman, *The Bible Unearthed*, New York: Touchstone, 2002

R. Grierson and S. Munro-Hay, *The Ark of the Covenant*, London: Weidenfeld and Nicolson, 1999

G. Hancock, *The Sign and the Seal*, London: Heinemann, 1992

M. Harel, *The Sinai Journeys: The route of the Exodus*, Los Angeles: Ridgefield, 1983

J. K. Hoffmeier, *Ancient Israel in Sinai: The Evidence for the authenticity of the Wilderness tradition*, New York: Oxford University Press, 2005

J. K. Hoffmeier, *Israel in Egypt*, New York: Oxford University Press, 1997

C. J. Humphreys, *The Miracles of Exodus*, London: Continuum, 2003

S. Kingsley, *God's Gold: The Quest for the Lost Temple Treasure of Jerusalem*, London: John Murray, 2006

S. Munro-Hay, *The Quest for the Ark of the Covenant*, London: I. B. Tauris, 2005

G. Phillips, *The Templars and the Ark of the Covenant*, Rochester, Vermont: Bear, 2004

R. Price, *Searching for the Ark of the Covenant*, Eugene, Oregon: Harvest House, 2005

A. F. Rainey and R. S. Notley, *The Sacred Bridge: Carta Historical Atlas of the Bible*, Jerusalem: Carta, 2005

L. Ritmeyer and K. Ritmeyer, *From Sinai to Jerusalem: The Wandering of the Holy Ark*, Jerusalem: Carta, 2000

L. Ritmeyer, *The Quest: Revealing the Temple Mount*, Jerusalem: Carta, 2006

R. R. Standish and C. D. Standish, *Holy Relics or Revelation*, Rapidan, Virginia: Hartland Publications, 1999

E. Ullendorff, *Ethiopia and the Bible*, London: Oxford University Press, 1968

I. Wilson, *The Exodus Enigma*, London: Weidenfeld and Nicolson, 1985

Wyatt Archaelogical Research, *The Ark of the Covenant*, Cornersville, Tennessee, 2005

Index

Aaron
    Death and burial   74–75
    Rod   20, 44, 74, 113, 200
    Sons   45, 114, 178
Abarim   81, 84–86
Abel-Shittim   86–88
Abihu   45
Abinadab   129, 136
Abu Ghosh   128–130
    Church of Our Lady, Ark of the Covenant   129–130
Abu Salih   155
Abu Tayi, Auda   54
Achor, Valley of   185
Adam   88
Aggadah   172
Ahio   136
Ai   100
Ain El Quiderat   48, 55, 65
Ain Musa   75
Aksum   154
    Chapel of the tablet   54
Al Qu'aida   56
Albright, William   96–97
Allenby Bridge   87–88
Altar of Incense   194
Alvarez, Father Francisco   159
Amalekites   37, 56, 62, 64
Amman   71
Amorites   62, 82–83
Anubis   23
Aphek   116
Aqaba   31, 35, 54, 69–72
Aqaba, Gulf of, *see* Gulf of Aqaba
Arabah, Wadi, *see* Wadi Arabah
Araq el-Emir   164
Araunah, threshing floor of   138
Ark of the Covenant
    Battery, *see* Battery, Parthian, in Baghdad
    Cherubim   21, 43, 45, 141–142, 163, 182
    Construction of   20, 43, 163
    In Denmark? *See* Bornholm Chapel

In Egypt? *See* Shishak
In England? *See* Burton Dassett hills and Napton-on-the-Hill
In Ethiopia? *See* Ethiopia, Ark of the Covenant in?
In France? *See* Rennes le Chateau
In Ireland? *See* Ireland, Ark of the Covenant in?
In Japan? *See* Japan, Ark of the Covenant in?
In Rome? *See* Romans, Ark taken by?
In Scotland? *See* Rosslyn Chapel
In Utah? *See* Mormon beliefs about Ark's location
In Islam   130–131
New Testament references   21
Radioactive source   45–46
Rod of Aaron, containing   20–21
Tablets of the law, containing   20–21
Arks generally, in ancient world   43–44
Arnon   81–82
Ashdod   118–121
Asherah   171–172
Ashkelon   105, 122
Assyrians, capture of Northern Kingdom by   161, 173
Aswan   161–161, 164–165
Auda Abu Tayi, *see* Abu Tayi, Auda
Axum, *see* Aksum
Azarias, *see* Kebra Negast

Baal   83, 171
Babylonians, conquest of Jerusalem by, *see* Jerusalem
Baldwin 1, King   157
Barak, Ehud   102
Baruch, Apocalypse of   182
4 Baruch,   182
Bashan   83, 95
Battery, Parthian, in Baghdad   45
Bayna-Lakhem, see *Kebra Negast*
Beckingham, Chris   11, 30, 40, 55, 58–60, 64–65, 136
Bedouin   43, 52, 54, 57, 61, 76, 82
Beit Shean   106
Bernard of Clairvaux   159
Beth (Beit) Shemesh   125–128, 177
Bethel   114
Bezalel   43
Blood of Jesus on Mercy Seat, *see* Chromosomes of Jesus
Bornholm Chapel   201
Breastplate, of High Priest   45–46, 177
'British Israelites'   187

Bubonic plague   120
Burckhardt, Johann Ludwig   54
Burning Bush   27–28, 29
Burton, Richard Francis   54
Burton Dassett hills   19, 178
Burton's Carpet Viper   78

Cairo   20, 22, 23
    Khan al Khalili   22
    Windsor Hotel   20, 22
Caleb   62, 63
Canaan, Land of
    Conquest of, see Conquest of Canaan
    Israelites, appearance of distinctive people in   107
    Relations with other states and areas   104–107
Cave of the Column   185
Chanukah, see Hannukah
Cherubim, see Ark of the Covenant
Chronicles, Second Book of   170, 172–173, 181
Chromosomes of Jesus   193, 194 –195
Church of Our Lady, Ark of the Covenant, Abu Ghosh, see Abu Ghosh
City of David, see Jerusalem
Cobra, Desert   78
Comode, Nelson   175
Conquest of Canaan
    Date of   95–97
    Generally   37, 93–108
Constantine   28
Copper Scroll   183–186
Cornuke, Bob   34
Crotser, Tom   182–183
Crusaders   70, 157
Cypriots, Canaanite trade with   106
Cyrus   175

Dagon   119–121
David, King   131, 136–138, 152, 162, 172–173, 179
Dead Sea   72, 73, 77, 81, 83, 88, 183
Desert animals, adaptation of   79–80
Desert Highway   71–72
Deuteronomy, Book of   37, 44, 99, 162–163, 172
Dhahiriya   170
Dhiban   82–83
Dibon-Gad   82–83
Dinnshenchas   187–189

Dome of the Rock, *see* Jerusalem
Doughty, Charles   54
Dumha na nGiall, *see* Mound of the Hostages
Dunam, definition of   105

Ebal, Mount, *see* Mount Ebal
Ebenezer   115–117
Eden   43, 45, 141
Edom   37, 64, 71–88
Egypt
    Canaan, relations with   106–107
    Magic in   45, 77
    Population of in Ramesside period   37–38
    Return of Ark to?   22, 169–171
Eilat   31, 69–72
Ekron   122–125, 127
Eleazar   114, 129, 131
Eleph   *38*
Elephantine Island   161, 164–165
Eli   115, 116–118
Elim   31
Enoch, Book of   182
Erlich, Ze'ev, *see* Jabo
Esdras, Second Book of   175
Essenes   183–184
Esther, Book of   165
Ethiopia   22, 149–166
    Aksum, *see* Aksum
    Axum, *see* Aksum
    Falashas, *see* Falashas
    Haile Selassie, Emperor, *see* Haile Selassie, Emperor
    Kebra Nagast, *see* Kebra Negast
    Lalibela, *see* Lalibela
    Prester John, *see* Prester John
    Timkat, *see* Timkat
Eupolemus   176, 179
Exodus
    Crossing of Re(e)d Sea   30–32
    Date of   95–97
    Numbers of Israelites   36–38
    Route   27–36, 47–48, 71–77, 80–89
    Sinai, evidence of in   47–48
Ezekiel, Book of   179, 197
'Ezekiel Code'   197
Ezion-Geber   31, 35, 54, 69–72

Ezra, Book of   176

Falashas   160, 165
Fat Sand Rat   80
Faust, Avi   12, 104–107, 122, 126
Feiler, Bruce   54
Feinan   77–81
Field's Horned Viper   78
Freemasons   158, 201, 202
Futterer, Antonia Frederick   182

Gabriel, Archangel, *see Kebra Negast*
Gamaliel, Rabbi   200
Garden Tomb, Jerusalem   22
Garstang, John   96
Gath   120–123
Gaza   106, 119, 122
Geoplasma   178
Getz, Rabbi   201
Gezer   105
Gibraltar   188–189
Gilgal   93–94, 104
Givat Yonah   118
Glassman, Lee   12, 99, 115, 118, 123, 125, 129, 136
Glory of the Kings, The, see Kebra Negast
Golden Calf   33, 44
Golden Spiny Mouse   80
Golgotha   32, 156
Gomorrah   32
Goren, Rabbi Shlomo   201–202, 208
Gothic architecture   158–159
Graves of Craving   57
Gulf of Aqaba   29–31, 32–34, 190
Gulf of Suez   31, 35

Hadiths   131
Haile Selassie, Emperor   154
Haj road, Sinai   35–36
Haman   165
Hancock, Graham   155, 156, 158–160, 164–166, 171
Hananiah, Rabbi   200
Hanukkah   160, 165
Hasban   84
Hatzor   105
Hazeroth   55

Hebron	47, 62, 63, 131, 170
Helena	28
Herskowitz, Esti	12, 100–101
Hertz, Rabbi	177
Heshbon	82–84
Hezekiah's Tunnel	197
Hill of Tara, *see* Tara, Hill of	
Hittites	62
Hivites	104
Hor, Mount, *see* Mount Hor	
Hophni	115, 117–118
Horn, Siegfried	183
Humphreys, Colin	37–38
Hyksos	95–96
Ichabod	118
Indiana Jones	169
Inter-marriage	85
Ireland, Ark of the Covenant in?	186–190
Islam, Ark of the Covenant in, *see* Ark of the Covenant	
Israelites, emergence as distinct people	104–107
Israelite temples outside Jerusalem	161, 164–165
Iye-Abarim	81
Jabbok	82
Jabo	101–103, 111, 113, 208
Jaffa	106, 199
Jamaluddin, Sheikh	131
Japan, Ark of the Covenant in?	177
Jebel el Lawz	32–34
Jebel Harun, *see* Mount Hor	
Jebel Madhbah	177
Jebel Musa, *see* Sinai	
Jebusites	62
Jeconiah	127, 129
Jehoiachin	173–174
Jehoiakim	173
Jeremiah	179–182, 186–190, 191
Jericho	86, 87, 94–98, 174, 185
Jerusalem	
Arrival of the Ark in	136–138
Ark of the Covenant still in?	22, 131
Assyrians, besieged by	173
Babylonians, conquest by	22, 145, 166, 174, 175–176
City of David	138

Dome of the Rock   139–145
Dominus Flevit, Church of   139
Garden Tomb, *see* Garden Tomb
Generally   98, 99, 115, 118, 199–200, 203–204
Gethsemane   139
Golden Gate   139
Kidron Valley   138, 139
Mount of Olives   139
Sakhra   144, 158, 199
Silwan   138
Tabernacle in   182, 200
Temple   21, 95, 135–136, 138, 140–144, 145, 155, 162–164, 170–176, 179–180, 182, 184–185, 207–208
Temple Mount   22, 138–145, 157–158, 188, 195, 197 et seq
Jesus, blood of, on Mercy Seat, *see* Chromosomes of Jesus
Jones, Indiana, *see* Indiana Jones
Jones, Vendyl   94, 183–186
Jordan, River   65, 81, 84, 88–89, 93, 94, 156
Jordan, State of   69–89
Joseph's Tomb   102, 103
Josephus   32, 85, 130
Joshua   47, 62–63, 85–88, 93–96, 100, 103–104, 106, 113
Josiah, King   143, 161–164, 171–173, 175
Judah, Kingdom of   161
Judas Maccabaeus   165, 181
Judges, time of   114 et seq
Juvelius, Valter Henrik   197–199

Kadesh Barnea   47–48, 64–65, 76
Kashrut, laws of   85
Kebra Negast   151 et seq
    Azarias   152
    Bayna-Lehkem, *see* Menelik
    Gabriel, Archangel   153
    Makeda   152
    Menelik   152
    Solomon, *see* Solomon
    Zadok   152
Kelt, Wadi, *see* Wadi Kelt
Kenyon, Kathleen   96, 97
Kibbutz Revadim   123
Kidron Valley, *see* Jerusalem
King's Highway   71, 72, 77, 81
Kiriath-Jearim, *see* Abu Ghosh
Knights Templar   19, 22, 157–160, 177–178, 199, 201

Kohathites   127–128
Koran   130

Lake Tiberias   131
Lalibela, city   156–157, 159
Lalibela, Prince   156, 159
Lawrence of Arabia, *see* Lawrence, T.E.
Lawrence, T.E   35, 51, 54, 71
Lehi   177
Leontopolis   165
Lia Fail   187
Loughcrew Passage Tombs   188–190

Maccabees, Second Book of   181–182, 185
Magic   45, 46, 77
Mahdi   130–131
Maimonides   200
Makeda, *see Kebra Negast*
Manasseh, King   169, 171–173, 180
Manna   20, 56–57, 129, 200
Marah   31
Masoretic text   127
Memar Marqah   130
Menelik, *see Kebra Negast*
Menorah   170, 175, 194
Merneptah stele   104–105, 106
Midian   29–35
Midrash   137
Midwives, Hebrew   36
Mishnah
     References to Ark in   200
     References to Tabernacle in   112
Mizpah   114
Mizpe Ramon   78–79
Moab   81–86, 95
Mormon beliefs about Ark's location   177
Moses   29, 33, 37, 40, 46, 55, 56, 58, 61–64, 71–75, 76–79,
                    83–86, 98, 130, 143, 162, 181, 202
Spring of, *see* Ain Musa
Mound of the Hostages   187–190
Mount Ebal   100, 102, 103
Mount Gerizim   100, 102, 103, 130
Mount Hor   74–75
Mount Horeb, *see* Mount Sinai
Mount Nebo   84–87, 182–183

Mount of Olives, *see* Jerusalem
Mount of Temptation   97
Mount Pisgah   85
Mount Sinai
    Jebel el Lawz   32–34
    Jebel Madhbah   177
    Jebel Musa   27–29
    Location   28–34, 76–77, 177
Mount Tsurugizan, *see* Japan, Ark of the Covenant in?
Myceneans, Canaanite trade with   106

Nabateans   70, 75–76
Nablus   100, 102–103, 130
Nadab   45
Napton-on-the-Hill   19, 178
Nathan   138
Nebi Musa   98–99
Nebo, Mount, *see* Mount Nebo
Nebuchadnezzar   174, 176
Nebuzaradan   174
Negev   29, 62, 74, 78, 85
Neuman, Silvie   12, 118–119, 121–124
Noah's Ark   32, 34
Numairi   177
Nuweiba   30, 32, 34

Obed-Edom   137
Ofra   101
Og, King   83
Old Cataract Hotel, Aswan, *see* Aswan

Parker, Captain Montague   198–199, 208
Petah Tikva   115
Petra   65, 73, 74–77
Petrie, Flinders   105
Phillips, Graham   76–77, 177–79
Philistines   21, 116–125, 127, 131
Phinehas   114, 115, 117
Pisgah, Mount, *see* Mount Pisgah
Pompey   175
Prester John   159
Price, Randall   202
Puah   36
Punon   77–81
Purim   160, 165

Pyramids	32
Qelt, Wadi, *see* Wadi Kelt	
Queen of Sheba	149, 151–152
Qumran	183–184
Rahab	95
Rameses II	96, 97, 105
Rath of the Synods	187
Ravens, Short-Tailed	76
Re(e)d Sea	30, 31
Rehoboam, King	170
Rennes le Chateau	201
Rephidim	31, 37, 62
Rift Valley, African	73
Ritmeyer, Leen	12, 144, 158
Romans, Ark taken by?	22, 175
Rosh Ha'Ayin	117
Rosslyn Chapel	201
Rum Wadi, *see* Wadi Rum	
St. Catherine's Monastery, Sinai	27–28
Burning Bush	27–28
St. George's Monastery, Wadi Kelt	97
Sakhra, *see* Jerusalem	
Samaria	100, 101, 111–113, 161
Samaritans	100, 130
Samuel	131, 137
Sanders, Michael	170
Sanpete Valley, *see* Mormon beliefs about Ark's location	
Saudi Arabia	29, 32–34, 71
Saul, King	131
Sauniere, Berenger	201
Sennacherib	173
Sepher Yosippon	182
Serabit el Khadem	35
Seventh Day Adventists	32, 196
Sharon, Ariel	202–203
Sheba, Queen of, *see* Queen of Sheba	
Shechem	100, 102–103, 130
Shekhinah	135, 203–204
Sheshonq I, Pharaoh, *see* Shishak, King	
Shikoku Island, *see* Japan, Ark of the Covenant in?	
Shilo(h)	104, 111–117, 163
Shiprah	36

Shishak, King   169–171, 180
Shittim, *see* Abel-Shittim
Sihon, King   82
Silwan, *see* Jerusalem
Sinai   27–32, 35–41, 47–65
    Birds   53
    Haj road, *see* Haj road
    Jebel Musa   27–29
    Mount Sinai, *see* Mount Sinai
    St. Catherine's Monastery, *see* St. Catherine's Monastery
    Travel in   51–65
Sisters of St. Joseph of the Apparition   129
Six Day War   201
Snakes   78–79
Sodom   32
Solomon, King 21, 95, 138–143, 149, 151–154, 155, 158, 159, 161,
                              170, 172, 173–174, 181, 199, 200
Spielberg, Steven   22
Spring of Moses, *see* Ain Musa
'Stones of Fire'   177–178
Subiaco   175
Suez, Gulf of, *see* Gulf of Suez

Taba   65, 70
Tabernacle   43, 45, 77, 111–112, 113, 127, 163, 175, 182, 185, 200
Table of Shewbread   170, 193, 194
Tacitus   175
Talmud   175, 201
Talmud Babli   175
Tamarisk   57
Tanis   188
Tara, Hill of   186–190
Teia   188–189
Tel Amarna tablets   106
Tel es-Safi, *see* Gath
Tel Gat, *see* Gath
Tel Hammam   87
Temple (Jerusalem), *see* Jerusalem
Temple Herdewyke   178
Temple Mount, *see* Jerusalem
Ten Commandments   41
Tiberias, Lake, *see* Lake Tiberias
Titus   175
Timkat   154
Tutankhamun   23

Utah, *see* Mormon beliefs about Ark's location
Uzzah   136–137, 178, 207, 208
Uzzi   130

Vatican   175
Virgin Mary
      As Ark of the Covenant   129–130

Wadi Arabah   72–81
Wadi Kelt   97–98
Wadi Rum   54
Warren, Charles   202
Warren's Gate   202, 203
Warren's Shaft   197
Wells, Peter   12, 196
Western Wall Tunnels   203
Wilderness of Zin, *see* Zin, Wilderness of
Williams, Larry   34
Wyatt, Ron   32–34, 190–197, 208

Yam suph, *see* Re(e)d Sea
Yanoam   105
Yemen   71, 151
Yitzhar   102–103

Zadok the Priest, *see Kebra Negast*
Zedekiah, King   174, 185, 188
Zered river   72, 81
Zias, Joe   12, 196
Zin, Wilderness of   77